Mrs. J. W. Stow

Probate Chaff

Or, Beautiful Probate

Mrs. J. W. Stow

Probate Chaff
Or, Beautiful Probate

ISBN/EAN: 9783337058487

Printed in Europe, USA, Canada, Australia, Japan

Cover: Foto ©ninafisch / pixelio.de

More available books at **www.hansebooks.com**

Mrs. J. W. Stow

PROBATE CHAFF;

OR,

BEAUTIFUL PROBATE;

OR,

THREE YEARS PROBATING IN SAN FRANCISCO.

A Modern Drama,

SHOWING

THE MERRY SIDE OF A DARK PICTURE.

BY THE AUTHOR OF
"PROBATE CONFISCATION."

"A little nonsense now and then,
Is relished by the best of '(wo)' men."

Illustrated
With something less than a Thousand Cuts of Historic Characters.

PUBLISHED BY THE AUTHOR,
AND SOLD BY SUBSCRIPTION,
PRICE $1.50.
1879.

Copyright, 1879,
BY
MRS. J. W. STOW.

TO

𝕭𝖊𝖆𝖚𝖙𝖎𝖋𝖚𝖑 𝕻𝖊𝖆𝖇𝖆𝖙𝖊

AND THE CAUSE OF

UNIVERSAL JUSTICE,

THIS VOLUME IS ADMIRINGLY

𝕴𝖓𝖘𝖈𝖗𝖎𝖇𝖊𝖉.

PREFACE.

Dear Readers:

You may search this book from beginning to end, and from the end to the beginning, with Mr. Weller's magnifying glasses, and you will not discover a particle of sense in it. You may winnow the chaff with the soft western zephyrs or the borean gales of the north, and you will get chaff, nothing but chaff, for your pains—believe me! Unless you have a stomach for trash don't read this book, for I have acted upon the advice which the old journalist gave the young journalist, who desired to know the secret of a successful newspaper. Said the wise old cool-head to the unwise young hot-head, "Make your paper trashy, if you want it to be popular; make it very trashy, make it *all* trash!"

Now this is exactly what I have done, and I am much obliged to the "cool old head" for his advice. I have written "Chaff" to please San Franciscans. When I offered them (some of them) "Probate Confiscation," they were not satisfied; their delicate appetites craved something more savory; they wanted "Helen's Babies" on toast or the "Innocents Abroad" on the half-shell. San Franciscans think I belong in shoal water, and that I was far out of my depth in "Probate Confiscation;" and to please them I have come ashore and am now in shallow, yes, more shallow, most shallow water, and I leave it to the readers of "Chaff" to decide whether I have found my natural element or not.

THE AUTHOR.

NEW YORK, May 21, 1879.

CONTENTS.

		PAGE
PROLOGUE	. . . .	ix

SCENE
- I. INTRODUCTION 11
- II. BEAUTIFUL PROBATE 34
- III. WANTED $10,000 57
- IV. I'VE GOT IT 81
- V. OPEN LETTER TO THE CHAMBER OF COMMERCE 103
- VI. LIVING IN THE CAVE 126
- VII. SEQUEL TO THE HISTORY OF A PET DOG . . 191
- VIII. SEASONABLE ADVICE TO WIDOWS . . . 205
- IX. JANE GILPIN'S PROBATE ASS 225
- X. TABLES TURNED 231
- XI. CONCLUDING REMARKS 260
- APPENDIX 287

PROLOGUE.

Thy splendor falls on widowed walls,
    And ancient pandects old and hoary;
Thy "*beauty*" breaks when morning wakes,
    And the "white Ermine" leaps in glory.
Blow, horruns, blow, set the merry *chaff* flying,
Blow, horruns, answer echoes, flying, flying, flying.
    Oh hush, Oh hear! how sweet and clear,
        And sweeter, clearer, farther going;
    Oh clear and far, from court and bar,
        The horns of *Probate*, gaily blowing!
Hark! Listen! the widows are replying;
"Blow, horruns, blow, send the *chaff* flying, flying.
    Oh, let it *sale* on every gale,
        O'er hill and plain, o'er field and river;
    And let it rise from earth to skies
        And float forever and forever.
Blow, horruns, blow, set the merry *chaff* flying,
Till every '*pleader*' answers, 'flying, flying, flying.'"

PROBATE CHAFF.

SCENE THE FIRST.

INTRODUCTION.

Omne ignotium pro magnifico.

INTRODUCING the author of this "*standard work*" to an appreciative and admiring public; introducing the "Probate Court," a beautiful institution! to an appreciative and admiring public, who, otherwise, would know but little about it, perchance, until they fall into it, and then they will know *all* about it. Beautiful Probate is an aristocrat. She belongs to one of the *old* families. She is as fresh as she was on the morning of her birth. Time can no more wither her than it could the "serpent of old Nile." Years but add to her strength. She slakes her thirst at the fountain of perpetual youth; men die and are forgotten, but beautiful Probate knows no death. She walks upright through the houses of death with a firm and haughty mien. But some day she will be felled to the earth by a blow from a *woman's* hand. Then no widows and fatherless children will be driven out of their homes into the barren pastures of the world—suffering the double death of financial ruin and social ostracism.

For the benefit of my numerous readers I will separate this beautiful court into its component parts and present them in the usual order of gradation, beginning with its immaculate head—the judge—the vicegerent of widows, the partitioner of dead men's estates, a stainless being robed in ermine and crowned with indisputable power; its ponderous body, which consists of a great standing committee of lawyers, whose numbers are as the leaves of the forest, unnumbered and numberless; its tail—it has a tail—*entail* (of horror to the initiated), composed of executors, appraisers, receivers, guardians, referees, clerks, auditors, reporters, publishers, bill-posters, auctioneers, cartmen, criers, citors, witnesses, and sheriffs. None of these men are ever paid five hundred dollars an hour or a day for their services—ah! no!

This great composite tail wags day in and day out, week in and week out, month in and month out, year in and year out, decade in and decade out, century in and century out, without money and without price. It wags solely for the love of wagging and for the love of the widows and the fatherless. Were it to cease wagging for an instant, this court, this beautiful Probate, would be in ruins. A dire calamity! A calamity that wrings the heart and takes one's breath away to think of!

However, be not deceived by fair words; this beautiful Court, Probate, is covered with a pall and has the odor of a charnel house; it is full of ghosts— the ghosts of dead hopes; it is mildewed with tears —the tears of widows and orphans; it is choked with sighs—the sighs of widows and orphans. It is a quiet court—this beautiful Probate. "No opposing crowds stimulate the legal warriors to torrents of invective, to flights of rhetoric, or shafts of wit." All that is necessary to secure a "*fat*" fee when the "clean up" comes, is for them to *look* into the court-room and tip a sly wink at the Ermine.

There is an old saw that says, "A still sow gets the swill." In this sense beautiful Probate is a still sow. Its wheels, pulleys, and cogs are kept so well and thoroughly greased by the gold of dead fathers and husbands, and the substance of widows and orphans, that they run as noiselessly as the dead sleep. It is a prosperous court. It does business on a large scale (*all* the property in the United States is filtered through it every *thirty* years). It never has any dull times, for it is in league with Death, who

THE WHITE ERMINE.

never tires, and whose old-fashioned weapon is keen and unerring. The harvest is always bountiful, and the beautiful Probate court is the granary. But I must analyze this beautiful institution and give it to you in detail; and I must also analyze my life during my three years *active* probating, and give it to you in detail.

Which shall it be? Shall the author take precedence of beautiful Probate, or shall beautiful Probate take precedence of the author? Toss up! Heads the author wins, tails beautiful Probate loses. Behold the result! *I* am victorious, for the *first* time, and shall proceed to transform myself into the third person *singular*. I always want to know all about my authors; you always want to know all about your authors—how they look, how they feel, how they act, what they eat, etc., etc. Now *you*, my dear reader, shall be gratified, although *I* am seldom or never, because most authors show up every-body's faces and foibles excepting their own.

Well! how shall I begin? Dear *me!* it isn't so easy after all. Where's my hand-glass? I've quite forgotten how I look. A historical circumstance. This won't do! I'm in slippers and have got a shawl on my head—in other words, I'm not "made up." If I were to paint myself as I am, you would not know me when you saw me. I must resort to some other expedient for a correct description. Well, well, well! let's see! Ah! I have it—my letter of credit—no, of exchange—no, of circulation—no, no, I don't mean either—I mean my letter of—of introduction to "*furrin*" lands—that's it, and here it is. How fortunate that it was not appraised with my other goods and chattels. It is written in French, but, fearing that your French may have got a little rusty from disuse, I will translate it: " Height, five feet seven; dress, black; uncertain age; inclined to *embonpoint;* common nose, dent in the chin, gray eyes, good teeth, sandy hair, sandy complexion, *sans* beauty." That's all. Now you will know me when you see me, which will be of great advantage, when there is nothing of importance to look at.

But how is this? I was to speak of myself as though I were not myself, but some other person. I was to introduce you to a third person singular, and here I have made the blunder of introducing you to a first person singular. Let us pause right here to get our bearings. We must resort to Murray, otherwise these *persons* will get inextricably mixed. "I, thou, he!" *He* is the third person, but this *third* person won't do. Try again! "I, thou, he, she, or it." It is third person, but *it* won't do. Try again! "I, thou, he, she"—Stop! *she*'ll do. *She* is the right third person singular.

When this third person singular was thrown into

this beautiful court, Probate, mentioned above, her deportment was *un*beautiful, so said the head, so cried the body, so swore the tail. This third person

NOT MADE UP.

singular said that she had never been in a court of justice (what of it?) and never wanted to be; said that this humane and equitable court, this beautful Probate, was not a whit better than the old Chancery court of England; said that she was a female Gridley, and that she, like he, had been forcibly cast into this consuming fire of a court when she was seven thousand miles away, on the peaceful shores of Geneva; said that the whole transaction smacked of feudalism, barbarism, and heathenism, and not of Christianity, progress, and enlightenment; said there was no more call for breaking up the home at the death of the father and husband, than there was at the death of the mother and wife; said that the beautiful Probate was a loathsome vampire which fattened on the vitals of the widow and the fatherless; said she would plead her own case, in open court, in spite of the displeasure of the white-ermined head, the disgust of the erudite body, and the contempt of the cringing tail.

She, this third person singular, cut such didos in the court-room, the beautiful Probate, and in the white-ermined judges' chambers, that all San Francisco stood on its head in amazement. She said that she would have her pet black and tan terrier, in spite of writs of replevin, sheriffs, deputies, police, and private detectives; in spite of paid thieves who sought to lasso him under her "common nose" in the street. She said that she would have her own hundred shares of Gilroy Consolidated—a Christmas gift from her husband—which stock the humane executors had taken away from her at his death and put with the other assets, playfully saying, "that a husband had no right to make his *own* wife a present—that it was not legal; that a gift from some other woman's husband is the only present that will hold legal water." Quite right! She further deposed and said, that with her single arm she would strike at this beautiful court, Probate, at its ermine-geared head, at its swollen body, at its remorseless tail, and all San Francisco, standing on its head, lifted up its voice, which was like the voice of Balaam's beast, and said, that she, this third person singular had gone raving mad—mader'n a bed-bug, March hare, or tempest—said that she "orter be ketched and shet up in a lunitic ass-lum;" said that she was more dangerous than a mad dog loose, for she stirred up strife in peaceful families, by preaching the double-dyed heretical doctrine that wives earn money, in their own households; said if it did not cost a "mint o' money" they would make up a purse and send her across the continent to Boston, among the other lunatics.

Returning to the first person singular, with your

permission, I will introduce the court, the beautiful court, Probate, or, rather its motor power *Probate Law*. I am well acquainted with Probate Law; we are one and indivisible, and have been for the last three years. Probate Law has been my protector, my shield, my—well, *not* support for the last three years, but we have paddled in the same canoe—all the same. Probate Law has been a husband to me ever since mine died, Probate Law is the universal husband of all widows, for a time—sometimes it is for a lifetime. The length of time Probate Law husbands widows is entirely owing to circumstances. If the widow is a "*fat*" widow—I mean by this, fat in purse, but not necessarily fat in person (the Unabridged definition of "fat" is duly laid down and embodied in the book "Probate Confiscation")—it is as long as the money holds out, usually. Probate Law does not meddle much with "*lean*" widows' estates—it is not worth while, you know. "Lean" widows are not, as a rule fascinating, widows—that is, their fascinations do not set the cogwheels of Probate Law in motion.

It plays some curious pranks, this Probate Law. It turns a widow out of her own home, wherein she may have toiled for forty years, at the end of forty days after the sods have hidden the face of the lover of her youth, the friend of maturer years, the father of her children. "What for?" you pertinently ask. For the financial protection of her husband's relations and her own children. She might be dishonest, you know, and sell the home, and with the money received from the sale she might buy "*gimp*" and other finery, to captivate another man, and thus beggar her children and her husband's relations, if good, *honest, disinterested* Probate Law did not step in and restrain her.

Probate Law is the universal guardian of all fatherless children. It never meddles with *motherless* children. Ah! no! motherless children are always beautifully taken care of. It protects the widow-mother in the right to nourish her infant, and to bring him through the dangerous period of mumps, measles, chicken-pox, rash, scarlet fever, and teething, but after these troublesome pitfalls in child-life are past, the most generous and humane Probate Law passes this child to a strange guardian, who has its interest so much more at heart than its own mother has. She is thus relieved of all further care of it. This beautiful legal provision is many—a great many—centuries old (Law, like wine, improves with age; the older it is, the better); it is executed in the name of universal *justice;* it is an unpruned outcropping of the universal care of the church in bygone ages. Buckle, in his "History of Civilization," speaking of church guardianship, says:

"The Scotch divines laid their rude and merciless hands on the holiest possessions of which our nature is capable, the love of a mother for her offspring. Into that sanctuary they dared to intrude; into that they thrust their gaunt and ungentle forms. If a mother held opinions of which they disapproved, they did not scruple to invade her household, and take away her children [a la Probate Court], and forbid her to hold communication with them. Or if, perchance, her own son had incurred her displeasure, they were not satisfied with forcible separation, but they labored to corrupt her heart, and harden it against her child [guardian and ward], so that she might be privy to the act. In one of these cases, mentioned in the records of the church of Glasgow, the Kirk-Sessions of that city summoned before them a woman, merely because she had received into her house her own son after the clergy had excommunicated him. So effectually did they work upon her mind, that they induced her to promise, not only that she would shut her door against her child, but that she would aid in bringing him to punishment. She had sinned in loving him; she had sinned, even, in giving him shelter; but, says the record, she promised not to do so again.

"She promised to forget him, whom she had borne of her womb, and suckled at her breast. She promised to forget her boy who had ofttimes crept to her knees, who had slept in her bosom, and whose tender frame she had watched over and nursed. All the dearest associations of the past, all that the most exquisite form of human affection can give or receive, all that delights the memory, all that heightens the prospect of life, all vanished, all passed away from the mind of this poor woman, at the bidding of her spiritual masters. At one fell swoop, all were gone; so potent were the arts of these men, that they persuaded the mother to conspire against her son, that she might deliver him up to them. They defiled her nature by purging it of its love. From that day her soul was polluted. She was lost to herself, as well as lost to her son. To hear of such things is enough to make one's blood surge again, and raise a tempest in our innermost nature."

To-day, in the white light of the nineteenth century, the Probate System stands in the same relation to the widow and the fatherless that the clergy did to the family in the middle ages. It clings so tenaciously to old forms and old customs, which had their birth in barbarism, that you will imagine when you get into this beautiful court, Probate, that you were born in eight hundred instead of eighteen hundred. If you are a widow, and I take it that you are, and an unsophisticated widow—one whose husband is just dead, and the cogwheels of *justice* have just begun to work—you will find that you can remain in your own home forty days without paying rent to beautiful Probate (magnanimous, isn't it?), but *not* without molestation; for the next day after the funeral you will have a call from the playful appraisers. First they will ask for your late husband's purse, sleeve-buttons, canes, linen-duster, umbrella, pistols, carpet-bag, watch and chain, private correspondence, and the family pet dog. When you have placed these things in a pile before them, they will put them in a bag—dog and all; then they will set a price on the handsome pictures, and stick a little "court" plaster of valuation on each in order to relieve their memory. Thus they will move on through the house of mourning, the house sacred to grief, ticketing everything of value; and when they go away they will take the bag with the watch and dog in it, and they will send a cart and take the pictures—the "valuable paintings"—and if you are a Scotch widow they will take your son and send him to Scotland to be educated, if your late husband thought that his mother could rear his son more to his—the dead man's—satisfaction than his son's mother could possibly do. And this is done in the name of universal justice and chivalric "protection."

At the end of the forty days, when you go out of your house and your trunks are placed on the sidewalks, they are at once pounced upon by the playful sheriff. The beautiful, consistent law does not allow them to be taken within doors, but the moment they touch pavement they are lawful plunder. "But why do they take my trunks?" you cry; "they contain all my jewels, laces, and wearing apparel." What of that? Beautiful Probate does not tolerate widows who are so unreasonable as to want to be housed, clothed, and fed. Your paraphernalia has gone to pay costs of court, madam. There was a time when paraphernalia was sacred and inviolable to the mourner, but that was a part of feudalism and has become obsolete.

You can repair the damages somewhat, you think, for you have money in the savings bank; but when you go to this beautiful institution for the protection of widows' funds, you are playfully informed that you cannot draw money out of the bank without an order from the court; and when you go for the order, the white-ermined judge puts you through a new kind of catechism and says:

"Is the money you wish to draw from the bank your separate earnings, or is it your late husband's money?"

"It is money that my husband gave me," you reply, "for *pin-money*, but he was liberal with me because he said I earned as much as he did in the care of the home, and in the bearing and the rearing of the children, and domestic duties generally."

"Ah! I see!" says the Ermine, significantly. "In law, my dear madam, that money is common property, and belongs to the estate. A husband cannot make direct gifts to his *own* wife."

"But," you plead, clinging to the last straw, "it was not a gift in reality, I had earned the money."

"No, no! madam!" bristles the Ermine, "a wife earns no money in wedlock; she is supported by her husband, and when he dies the property he has earned goes by natural entail to this court, this beautiful Probate, which has been stricken with chronic consumption since the moment of its birth. It consumes all the '*fat*' of dead men's estates." "What for?" you ask. "What for, madam? So that philanthropy may not die of inanition; so that the condition of the widow and the fatherless, made paupers by this beautiful court, may stir the tender public heart to heroic deeds."

But there is consolation for you yet. You will find all your old friends with their hats off and their palatial homes wide open to receive you. You will find the grave of your husband, who was a philanthropist, heaped with floral offerings. You will find that your minister, and your minister's wife, and your minister's daughter—now that you are homeless and poor—will redouble their attentions, that they will show by their many acts of kindness that they practice their own precepts. And you will further find that acquaintances who have been warmed and fed at your fireside have been stricken with *myopia* —a mild sort of epidemic which is not incurable. You will find, when you tell the clerk at the *Bon Marché* that he can charge that two yards of crape to account, that he moves away to look up the proprietor—who is not *in* at the moment, or is *lost* in the basement—and then he, the tapeman, returns sorrowful, rueful, and disconsolate, and folding up the two yards of weeds tells you that he, personally, does not trust, for he is a poor young man with large expectations.

"But how is this?" you exclaim with flashing

eyes (waste powder), " I have been trusted thousands of dollars here?"

"Can't help it!" the *not* obsequious tapeman replies, "them's th'orders frum the boss," and he—tapeman—hums to himself a fragment of Black Crook, while he drums an accompaniment with his fingers on the counter, and keeps time with his toes on the floor. You pay for the two yards of crape because it has been cut off, but you never cross that dry goods threshold again—not even in after years when times have changed, and you drive past in your elegant carriage and the "found" proprietor stands grimacing and ducking within the door. You are wiser now, by some years and varied experience, than you were on that sad morning in your young widowhood.

Some day you will see a woman sailing down the street dressed in the very latest fashion, and smelling of bergamot—a Christian woman who had always "*sistered*" you before your husband's death, because she had none of her own, and it was so nice to have a dear sweet sister by adoption. The moment this "meek and lowly" creature sees her "adopted" before her in a faded gown and old gloves she dashes round a corner, up another street, and you dash after her, and laying your hand in no gentle manner on her arm, sheathed in fresh silk, say, "Madam, what if we should meet in heaven?" But this sweet-scented, sainted "sister" shakes you off as though you were a viper—as she hisses "*Impossible!*"

You will soon learn that an order from this beautiful court, Probate, is needed for everything. If you want to make a hasty pudding for the children's supper you will find it a slow coach before you get through with it, for you have got to "show cause" why you desire to mix Spring Valley and corn-meal, before you can get the order. If you desire to sneeze, the white-ermined judge must hold your nose during the performance. If you have the toothache, no dentist will jeopardize his profession by looking at it—the tooth, not the ache, without an order from the beautiful court, stamped with the great seal of the Ermine.

You must never get sick while you are a Probate widow, because beautiful Probate does not countenance any such indiscretion on the part of its widows. It reasons, and reasons well, that health is the normal condition of humanity—and it fosters nothing which is abnormal (but itself). If you want a new gown, or a pair of shoes, or a nightcap—you will have to take all your old gowns, and old shoes, and old night-caps, to the chambers of beautiful Probate, to be inspected by the white Ermine, and if he finds that the gowns are not rent, and the old shoes have soles, and the night-cap strings are unbroken, he reads you a lesson on frugality, and you depart without the order. If the baby needs a bib, its gums have to be felt by the white Ermine, and its cut teeth counted, ere he will issue an order for the drooler; and when you read the order, it calls for a *rubber* bib. "Why rubber?" Because it saves soap. Beautiful Probate is economical with widows, and with widows' teething babies.

You will find, if you are a Connecticut widow, if you are too poor to support your children, that beautiful Probate can imprison you for the failure; and you will find, if you are a divorced mother—"a *grass widow*"—in Wisconsin, that you will be thrown into jail for secreting your child, so that the beautiful court cannot playfully take him from you and give him to your some-time husband, who suffered so much at the birth of this child! and whose nights were consumed in the care of it during its early infancy! And you will further find, if your home is in Pennsylvania—that you have no *legal* right to the *dead* body of your husband. It is the property of his kindred. There are a great many other "*findings*," in the sunless labyrinths of beautiful Probate, that I will generously leave covered so that you may enjoy the pleasure of the "*surprise*," when they are revealed to your unsophisticated vision.

In the following chapters I shall take my own case for a "precept and example"—a three-years case of probation, and active probating. I shall tell you how, during those three years, I went to court, to beautiful Probate, many times each week, to look at its white-ermined head, to listen to its plethoric body—and to watch its cringing tail. I shall show you, in part, how I lived, and what I did during those three years that I was in this beautiful Probate—I am still in Probate, or, my case is rather, my body is in Gotham at this writing, but my case is in the beautiful court, Probate—which particular court is situate in the city by the bay, in the land of the setting sun.

I give you my court history, believing that mine is *instar omnium*, and that some others may profit by my delightful and varied experience. Believe me! I shall seek to give you electric light upon the charming subject of Probates in general, and this one in particular—of the fascinations of high (garret) life in beautiful Probate. I shall be as zealous in carrying about and holding up to view my court-lantern of experience as old Cæsar was his midnight lantern of investigation, and I trust that mine will shed forth as brilliant a light in the domain of beautiful Probate as his did in the domain of Plutonian darkness.

Old Cæsar was an ancient gentleman of color, who lived in Boston in the year of our Lord 1769. "At that time, owing to the presence of disorderly persons and the delicacy of the midnight watch, they—the midnight watch—were ordered by the chief to patrol two together, and to arrest all gentlemen of color ('because they intensified the darkness,' I suppose) found after dark without a lantern. Soon after old Cæsar was picked up prowling about in total darkness. The next morning, when asked by the magistrate if guilty, he answered, 'No sah! I has de lantun'—holding up before the astonished court *an old one* innocent of oil or candle. He was discharged, and the law amended so as to require a lantern with a *candle* in it.' But old Cæsar was soon up again on the same complaint, and again entered the plea 'Not guilty!' and drawing forth the same old lantern, triumphantly exhibited an entire candle, whose tufted wick was as white as the eyes of its owner. He was discharged with a sharp reprimand, and the law was again tinkered so that it read 'a lantern with a *lighted* candle in it.' Old Cæsar was not up again, 'for,' said he, 'Massa's got too much lite on de subjec'."

Now this is exactly what I desire to have upon the "subjec'," for there cannot be too much "lite" on the "subjec'" of beautiful Probate. It must be seen and felt to be appreciated. One must have lived long years in its effulgent light and tender embrace to be a *just* judge of its merit. It makes one of a lively temperament very lively. If one is possessed of a speculative turn of mind, it excites effort and enterprise; if one is inclined to humanitarianism it calls out all their philanthropic nature, and invests them in a halo of their own glory and general importance. This was the direction in which beautiful Probate tenderly led your author.

SCENE THE SECOND.

BEAUTIFUL PROBATE.

Ubi mel, ibi apes.

AFTER much careful thought on the captivating subject, my dear readers, I have decided to introduce to your admiring eyes *my* beautiful Probate—in detail, and *my* white Ermine—in detail. I regret to inform you that you will have to be satisfied with a pen and ink sketch of his *Honor*, unless you accompany me to the court in person—as I shall now cordially invite you to do. Alas! that I should have no picture of my Ermine excepting the one so deeply engraven on my heart. But you shall go with me and get his impress stamped on your hearts as well.

Come, then! We will proceed as carefully, if you please, as though we were treading on incubating eggs, and as softly as though we were in a house full of babies.

First of all I must describe the building in which my beautiful Probate holds forth, and in which my white Ermine is enthroned. This I shall do in detail, also, for the benefit of those who do not accompany me. It is a corner building—corners on Kearney and Washington Streets. It does not pride itself on its architectural grandeur, but what it lacks in magnificence it makes up in site. It sees a great deal (of misery and heartache). A lovely plaza filled with evergreens and swallows is in front of it; above and around it is the air—a great body; below it is made ground where the waters of the Bay used to moan and sob; now the widow and the fatherless moan and sob within it; over against the western horizon is "Knob Hill," and within smelling distance the Chinese quarters.

There is a front entrance and a back entrance to my beautiful Probate. Widows in full-fleece go in at the front and go out at the back—shorn. *Ye special Probate pleader* comes in at the back, shorn, and goes out at the front in full-fleece.

As you who have accepted my invitation are unshorn, as yet, we will enter at the front portal and go along the broad passage and up the stairs. Step cautiously, for *they* are not very broad nor very well lighted. The sun gets faint and discouraged at their foot, and makes no effort to mount higher. We have arrived at the top landing. The air is stifling, but perseverance will bring us to the middle door, on the right of the contracted hallway, whose shadowy outlines we see through the gloaming.

Here we are! Pause and uncover (if you wear a hat)! We are about to enter and stand on consecrated ground—ground consecrated to the widow and the fatherless. Lay your hand reverently on the knob of the door. Sacred, historic door! Door of the widow's ark, *beautiful Probate*. Built of no costly material thy posts are not inlaid with pearls and precious stones—no Ophir's gold adorns thy panels. Heart of pine art thou—pine that grew in the primeval forest of Oregon. Soft and tender are thy fibres—easy to puncture as the ermined-heart within. Beautiful door! thou art dearer to the widow's heart than forests of oak—more fragrant than wildernesses of sandalwood, more precious than groves of rosewood and mahogany.

Enter! *Ecce homo!!! My* Ermine! An invisible nimbus floats above his head — a half circle of concentrated widow benedictions. My Ermine is tall and thin, and not *very* handsome. But this deficiency is more than balanced by suavity. He is very suave if you don't offend him. He has steel gray eyes that glitter behind his glasses (he wears glasses) like diamonds in the dark. He has a long, narrow head, a sort of two-story arrangement, and the top of the top-loft is as bare as a plucked bird —and shines like the heart of a poppy. A tornado of thought has lifted out every hair by the roots. His harmonious nose is long and narrow, in keeping with his head. His lips are thin, and his teeth well made. He wears a white vest, and a gold chain, and bob over it—and diamond studs in his dickey. His coat, and pantaloons, and boots are of the latest fashion, and cut straight. His hat is silk—and his handkerchief is silk, and his stockings are silk—and I have no doubt but that he wears other *unmentionable* silk-gear—and his manner is silky, and his smile, when he is not ruffled, is as soft as that pliant fabric. He is a widower—strange to relate. Then, again, not at all strange, for his heart is too tender to show partiality. Could he marry *one* widow, only, and leave all the other widow aspirants for his hand to pine in secret "like worms i' the bud?" No, never!

I feel no delicacy in thus having described my Ermine—at full length—for great geniuses in exalted positions are public as well as private property. They are the blazing beacons on the mountain-tops of inspiration. The heroes of peace and good order, and prosperity. My hero has inspired me to write *Probate Confiscation.* The book of books. It is illumined by the lamp of reason—whose oil is perpetually replenished by a constant stream from the widow's *cruse* (of wrath)—held by the hand of an admiring present, and it will continue to be replenished through all the years to come—by the hand of a grateful and admiring posterity.

THE BOOK OF BOOKS.

Look at him! The Ermine! seated on the throne of beautiful Probate. What magisterial dignity! and what a ravishing pose. This particular kind of throne is called a "*bench,*" but it is no bench at all, in the usual acceptation of the term. It is a soft-cushioned chair—padded and stuffed with *male* votes. This soft-padded chair has three feet—like an inverted trident, instead of four. It revolves on an emblematic screw, and it has the appropriate motto—"All manner of turning and twisting done here."

This throne, or bench, or chair, or revolver, is the terror of widows and orphans—that is, to the initiated ones. This shows the stupidity and want of forethought in widows and orphans, particularly the former, who ought to have profited by years of experience. In reality, beautiful Probate is most merciful to widows. For, were it to leave them in undisturbed possession of the fortunes that their defunct lords

BEAUTIFUL PROBATE'S REVOLVER.

left them, they would have no peace of their lives. They would be beset by suitors from morning till night. Portia's persecutions would sink into insignificance beside rich widows. It would not matter how *old* or how *fat* they were, if they were only financially plethoric. Beardless youth and toothless age would rival ripe manhood in zeal to become "protectors," the "*oaks*," for these torn vines to cling to.

Permit me to introduce my special pleader. He, too, is tall and lean, and wiry, and chews tobacco, and smokes a pipe. That will do for the present. The opposing pleader is—well, a friend to widows. I need not describe him.

The executors of my husband's (and my) estate, occupy those two chairs at the right of the scribe. Look in their faces, and you will read as in a book —(*Probate Confiscation*) uprightness. Look at their hands, and observe how clean and white they are. Look at their straight and narrow feet. Feet never found in forbidden paths. By the window nearest the Ermine, a widow, in " billows of crape," is holding by the hand a fair-haired boy, and weeping bitterly. She is young, and pretty, and *clinging*, therefore every tear will count with his " Honor." But woe to the old, and ugly, and stiff-jointed widows!

The fair-haired boy, that the young mother in her first grief holds by the hand, so lovingly—looks wonderingly at the white Ermine, at the back of beautiful Probate's revolver—at the shrewd face of the witness in the chair, at the left of the revolver, and at the special pleader, Mr. Pumpum, who is cross-examining the witness.

Mr. Pumpum resembles the cedars of Lebanon, and the oaks of Bashan in height, being seven feet three inches in his cotton socks. His visage is far from prepossessing, being of that jaundiced hue peculiar to underdone pie-crust. The hot flame of his intellectual furnace has singed off all the stubble on top of his head—excepting a diminutive forelock.

MR. PUMPUM.

But as a sort of compromise, a short, grizzly fringe of hair crops warily out above the long ears and below the brain-hemisphere. Mr. Pumpum is so tall, and the witness-chair is so low, owing to the short joints between floor and ceiling, that when he rises to his full height, he looks down on the terrified witness in much the same fashion that a hawk looks down on the dove, ere it makes the deadly swoop. Look at him! standing there with arms tightly folded, and his body slightly bent forward in pointer-like eagerness, to catch every sound and observe every motion of the sworn victim in the chair.

Whatever an ordinary witness has got in him is sure to come out when this keen-tonguesman gets hold of him. But the sharp, wide-awake, alert lady before us is not of the ordinary stamp. She has sat in the witness-chair before to-day, and she has seen just such special pleaders as Mr. Pumpum before to-day. She is not subdued by his insolence nor the Ermine's frowns. Her wits are well-sharpened on the whetstone of experience, and they never desert her. They stand her in good stead as a body-guard. Listen to the germane questioning.

Mr. PUMPUM. Where do you reside when at home, madam?

WITNESS. You-be-dam, sir.

Mr. P. Is it a long distance from here?

W. About the length of your understanding.

Mr. P. On which side of the street in You-be-dam do you live?

W. On either side.

Mr. P. How is that? Be careful, don't perjure yourself, madam.

W. If you go up it's on the right; if you come down it's on the left.

Mr. P. What did you have for breakfast this morning?

W. None of your business.

Mr. P. Was it cold or hot?

W. Hot.

Mr. P. Did you drink coffee or tea with it?

W. Coffee.

Mr. P. Do you *swear* on oath that it was coffee?

W. No.

Mr. P. Why did you tell me it was coffee, then?

W. I bought it for coffee, but it may have been chickory and beans.

Mr. P. Was the coffee, or chickory and beans, in a bowl, or cup and saucer?

W. In a cup.

Mr. P. Was there anything in the cup before you poured in the coffee?

W. Yes.

Mr. P. What was it?

W. A spoon.

Mr. P. Did you have sugar or milk, or both, in the coffee?

W. Sugar.

Mr. P. Did you stir the coffee and sugar with your finger and lick it afterwards?

W. I stirred the beverage with a teaspoon and my finger, aided and abetted by the thumb on the same hand as the finger.

Mr. P. Why did you do that?

W. Because a teaspoon don't stir of its own volition.

Mr. P. What else did you have besides the coffee?

W. A lamb chop, broiled.

Mr. P. Was the lamb that furnished the chop a blooded animal or a common sheep?

W. A commoner. No patrician blood flowed in its veins. It was a democrat.

At this thrust the learned council winced and the bystanders giggled, for Mr. Pumpum was a red-hot political ranter and "a *dimocrat.*"

With a violent effort Mr. Pumpum swallowed the smoke of his anger, and thus continued:

"What is your name, madam?"

W. Ask the clerk.

CLERK. Her name is Ophelia Clapp. *Mrs.* Ophelia Clapp, sir.

Mr. P. Is Clapp your *real* name, madam?

W. Clapp, sir; Clapp *is* my *real* name—my husband's *real* name is Clapp——

"Confine yourself, madam, to answering the direct and *important* questions," said the Ermine, with a two-edged glance at the undaunted witness.

Mr. P. Did you court Mr. Clapp, or did Mr. Clapp court you?

W. Ask Clapp.

Mr. P. What sort of people do you associate with, Mrs. Clapp?

W. All sorts—from lawyers up. Again the great unwashed outside the railing tittered, and Mr. Pumpum, losing the balance of his equanimity, roared:

"Mrs. Clapp, you've got brass enough in your face to make a twelve-quart kettle." "Yes," she replied, "and you've got sass enough in your head to fill it," at which the court joined in the laugh, to the strong disapproval of the "bench." Mr. Pumpum, to conceal his wrath, took from his coat-tail pocket a red bandanna handkerchief and blew a tuneful blast on his nose, which organ immediately took on the hue of the bandanna. Order being restored, Mr. Pumpum decided to suspend the cross-examination of the witness in the chair until this day six months, and Mrs. Clapp, with a smile to the court and a bow to the bench stepped down from the chair, which is immediately filled by a tousle-headed Irishman, with a nose like Prester John's foot, and a mouth like the crater of Vesuvius. The clerk (I'm going to describe this functionary and his brother functionary, the scribe, who is writing on a music-stand over in the corner there, when I get through with the witnesses, special pleaders, and cross-examiners) at once proceeds to swear the gentleman, by saying something, or mumbling something, that sounds just like " gwumble, gwumble, gwumble," as though his mouth was full of hot "*puddun.*" The son of Erin kisses the " book " (which, between you and I, is an old copy of negro minstrels' songs—so I was told, in all confidence, by a special pleader), and looks as much at home in the chair as a duck in a puddle.

Mr. P. What is your name?

W. Michael McClinches. What's yourn?

Mr. P. John Flaherty.

W. John Flaherty, is it? *Faix!* Did ye luse the O in the sae coomin' over? fur whin I node yez in owld Erland yez had an *O* ter yer name, bigger ner a kart-whale.

At this unlooked-for retort, Mr. Pumpum looks daggers, while he performs another sonata on his nose, in the red bandanna. At the close of the performance he speedily recovers himself, all but his musical organ, which is rapidly turning from crimson to purple, with indignation. But, in spite of the tell-tale member, Mr. Pumpum continues the cross-examination as though he had not been thrown off his guard, by saying—"Where were you born?"

W. Bliss God! not ten feet from yer fathers own door in Killarney, where we wuz b'ys togither.

Mr. P. Where were you educated?

W. I'm a gragawate o' Dooblin Univarsity, as well as yersilf.

Mr. P. Are you married?

W. Yis.

Mr. P. Did your wife bring you anything?

W. Yis.

Mr. P. What?

W. A *mother-in-law*.

Are you not tired of listening, my dear reader? I am. Let us look about a bit, and rest our overstrained mentality. Do you see that door at the left of the witnesses' chair? Within that door is the white Ermine's den, or, in strict court parlance, "*chambers*," a little long coffin of a room. I have been in that room, or *those* "chambers," many and many a time, to the great annoyance and disgust of the Ermine. I never was a raving favorite of his "Honor's." There, in there, I have seen him sign thousands of papers, which he never *once* looked at, as cheerfully as though he were signing his own death-warrant. Simple folk think he knows all about what he is doing, and knows every case by heart. With such confiding people "where ignorance is bliss, 'tis folly to be wise," perhaps.

Come this way. Step carefully, or you will be upset by the spittoons. They occupy nearly all the standing room. I counted forty, one day, when I had got tired of admiring the Ermine, without the scribes. It smells bad in here. Let us go through the little gate in the railing that separates the great unwashed from the court, and move along, through the mass of curious or interested humanity, until we find ourselves in the outer-court, or anteroom. Sit down on this bench, the widow's "*anxious seat*," and I will tell you something in all confidence. Through that door, over there by the table with the pitcher on it—is a room full of clerks and pigeon-holes—and every pigeon-hole has the will of a dead man in it, and there are a million holes.

One afternoon I came here—*in this very room*—and sat down at that table with the pitcher on it, and requested the privilege of looking at J. W. Stow's will. You are allowed to *look* at your deceased husband's will, but you are not allowed to remove it, or any of its paper guards from beautiful Probate. It was late when I came in on this particular occasion; the court closes at four, I had been selling *Probate Confiscation*, and had been so fascinated with the charming occupation and with the charming people who bought it, that I had taken no notice whatever of the flight of time. But, as I was saying, it was very late, and just as I had got to the pith of my investigations, Mr. Clerk pounced down upon me and said, "*Time's up.*" Then he walked back to his desk with all the lofty swell which characterizes beautiful Probate's officials. While his back was toward me, and his face turned to the opposite window, I embraced the opportunity, and, seizing time by the forelock, slipped into one of my many concealed pockets, the paper that contained the information sought— which, I confess, was a slippery piece of business. I knew I was breaking the peace and defying the law, but what of it, so long as the end was gained?

I kept the document out of sheer—what?—cussedness, for several days after I had extracted the desired information. Then I took it back, and with malice aforethought, I demurely handed it to the clerk, simply saying, "I was so late the other day, I was obliged to take this paper home." I could have called for the whole package of documents, and replaced this one unobserved, while ostensibly examining the others, but that was not my purpose. Mr. Clerk had shown too much feather for that; I intended to astonish him, and my intentions were not frustrated.

Seizing the paper, he unfolded it, and his gimlet eyes ran eagerly up and down the written matter. The chirography was not very *prononcé*. It was in a lawyer's hand, and resembled the footprints of migratory flies after an ink bath. When he had fully persuaded himself that the paper was really a *Stow Estate* document he bestowed a look of terror and indignation and wrath on me. How he must have cursed himself at that awful moment for being such a runt, for after standing on tiptoe he had to look up to see my face. Laying hold of the back of a chair, in order to steady himself on his toes, he opened his mouth with a gasp, and here is what came out of it:

"Goodness sakes alive! Mrs. Stow, you didn't take this paper home, I hope?" "Certainly I did," I coolly replied; "what of it?" "Didn't you know it was agin the law to remove probate documents from the court?" he continued, with a demi-semiquaver in his voice. "I didn't doubt that fact," I responded, with a sweet smile, "when I surreptitiously possessed myself of the paper." "Then why did you do it?" he fiercely exclaimed, teetering up and down on his toes and frothing at the mouth. "I have told you why," said I, nonchalantly; "I wanted to decipher the hieroglyphics that embellish it, and I hadn't time to do it here, but I had time to do it at home."

"You mustn't do it agin, madam," he continued, dropping on his heels and folding the paper with set teeth. "What would happen to me if I should do it again?" I meekly asked. "You would be subject to a fine, madam, and possibly sent up—*up*" (with a curdling emphasis on the last *up*). "Do you *understand?*" "Not quite. What does '*up*' signify in beautiful Probate parlance?" "Imprisonment, madam; bread and water, stone floors and grates." "I hope the grates have fires in them, for stone floors are apt to be damp in San Francisco," I musingly said, and with a bland smile I bowed myself out of the little august presence.

"Why don't you describe *him*, in detail, as you promised to?" you impatiently exclaim. "But," I reply, "you should have reminded me of the omission before. It is too late now. However, there is little lost, for there's little to paint even with so small a brush as the point of a steel pen. He is larger than a yearling baby, and smaller than Hercules. But what is lacking in stature is made up in pomp. He is very pompous. When you go to San Francisco, go and see him while you are visiting the other curiosities. I will give you a passport to beautiful Probate, and then you can see my Ermine and the scribe, and that will save me the trouble of describing the scribe. You need not be familiar with every face in the picture to appreciate its excellence, and enjoy its beauty."

Bear in mind, gentle reader, that I am addressing two audiences. Those who are with me in court, and see with their own eyes, and those whose duties detain them at home, and, per consequence, whose vision must be through another's lens.

Hark! they've shut up shop inside. Let's peek through the keyhole and see what they are about. What ails the Ermine? He is spinning round on the revolver like a top, and do look at Pumpum, with his feet among the inkstands and volumes on the table, and his head in a volume of tobacco smoke, and *do* look at the clerk and scribe, *minueting* over there in the northwest corner. How lively they "*cuterdown.*" You could roll marbles on their coat-tails. Look! *quick*. See those two special pleaders wrestling. There they go, neck over heels, into the spittoons. The biggest one has got the claret spigot loose in his nose. *My!* how high he must live to be so full of red current.

Crash! There goes a pane of glass. Well, never mind that, there will be one pane less in this temple of pains.

"Who broke it," do you ask? Can't you see who did it? Look sharp! Some of the merry pleaders are playing battledoor and shuttlecock on the side of the table next the window, and when the white Ermine is not rotating he is tallying the bouts.

What is that you say? "You supposed that the members of the bar were a dignified, decorous set." Why, my dear unsophisticated darlings, this is nothing in comparison to what the great body, the *élite* of the profession do at their state dinners over in Merchant Street. When the terrapin and champagne get in, the dignity and decorum get out, and then what follows? They lay aside all restraint and play leap-frog, pick-a-back, and hang the quail; they somersault, blind man's buff, and scotch the weasel; they perform every trick known to freemasonry. Dignified judge and learned pleader, each in his turn plays goat. These are facts that I gleaned from the Erebus who serves them.

One charming morning I strolled into the gorgeous

Bacchanalian apartments on Merchant Street, in quest of *Probate Confiscation* customers. At the moment I entered these " festive halls," there was no one there on guard, but I at once made myself at home, as I usually do among beautiful surroundings, and feasted my eyes to my heart's content on the substantial and artistic adornments; the spotless linen of the long table extending the whole length of the grand saloon; the polished china, cut glass and pure (none o' yer plated) silver; the gorgeous upholstery; the exquisite chandeliers, with their thousand prismatic pendants; the rich, lace-lined curtains and soft carpets; the beautiful pictures on the tinted walls; the frescoed ceilings and graceful statuary. Passing a mirror in my enjoyable "go-round," for I had kept " moving on," I was startled to find myself shadowed by a bronze Apollo, who moved when I moved and stood still when I stood still.

Don't be alarmed, dear friends and readers! It was not the one on a pedestal in the corner. It was Erebus, the handsome ebony servitor. How long he had shadowed me I know not. As soon as he saw a strange creature in petticoats, with a satchel in her hand in the room, he had evidently felt it incumbent upon him, as a counter of the spoons and statuary, to follow, follow, somewhat after the fashion that his brother-in-color followed a French lady and her cat on he Vallejo steamer, once upon a time, when Mr. Stow and I and little Gyp were going to the "White Sulphur." The lady had concealed her pet, as she thought, under her shawl, but the long tail of the Angora streamed like a white pennant behind, so that she, her *chère ami* and their intensified shadow, caused any amount of merriment among the non-dyspeptic passengers. That graceful appendage cost my lady a four-bit piece ere the boat touched the wharf at Vallejo.

As soon as *my* shadow saw that I saw him, and he saw the startled expression on my face, he quickly changed his position, and coming to the front with a polite bow (there is not a nation that can successfully compete with the African in a graceful salutation), said, "Beg pardon, missus! Is you a woman lawyah? 'Cos if you ain't, you're not 'lowed in heah. Dis is de lawyahs' club-room." "And a very beautiful room it is, too," I replied. "What do the members do after dinner?" I questioned, and then followed the *denouement* which I have just rehearsed for your delectation.

Now that you have been formally introduced to *my* beautiful Probate and to *my* white Ermine, and the upright executor's, there will be firm ground between us, and we need not remain in this close room any longer. I must take you into the *free* air and sunlight, which no Probate alchemist can bottle up. We descend the stairs and stand in the street with something of the feeling which Dante had when he left the last circle of the Inferno, and came where he could see the stars again.

You will find the real grain and pith of *my* probate experience in *Probate Confiscation*. It is too serious to mix up in these chaffy pages. But *Probate Confiscation* is still for sale, and no library is complete without it.

AN UPRIGHT EXECUTOR.

Buy a copy. *Probate Confiscation* and *Probate Chaff* are inseparable correlatives and should not be separated.

However, the following scenes will sunlight forth the bursting bubbles on the shores of beautiful Probate—the drifting foam on a sea of troubles. And "*Chaff*" shows which way the wind blows.

SCENE THE THIRD.

WANTED, TEN THOUSAND DOLLARS.

Ad præsens ova cras pullis sunt meliora.

In the early days of my charming probate experience, I was seized with an irresistible desire, a philanthropic impulse, as it were, to build two houses on two vacant lots which I own and possess, on Sacramento Street, in the city and county of San Francisco. "Yes," I said to myself, confidentially, "I will build two houses—*twins*—and they shall be as like as two peas in one peasecod; joined and cemented at their sides as inseparably as were the Siamese Twins, and I will say to the architect:

> Build them straight, O worthy master,
>   Staunch, and strong ; a noble structure
> That shall laugh at all disaster—
>   Laugh at winds and earthquake rupture.

"Within these *redwood mansions* there shall be a place for everything. Nothing shall be forgotten.

There shall be a closet for pies, and a buttery for cheese; a nook for boots and a nail for the jack; a chest for linen, and a cubbyhole for bottles; a hearth for the cricket, and a wall for the cockroach; a garret for spiders and a cellar for rats. Here the blushing bride shall be brought, in lace and orange blossoms, and installed mistress in each charming house, one for each; here the first baby shall be born, which baby will look just like papa, with mamma's eyes; but nose, chin, and complexion *just like papa's,* for all the world; here children shall gambol without restraint, and old age repose in peace; here flowers of rarest dies shall clamber over walls and enwreath the pillared door-ways; here the wild bird shall build her nest and rear her young; here every zephyr wafted through the Golden Gate shall bear health and beauty on its pinions, and every fog-banner shall unfurl a silver lining; here peace and plenty shall go hand in hand, and gaunt-eyed want shall never enter. But where shall I get the money to build these Arcadian homes? Where? Eureka! I have it! I will go to Thistle—Thistle has the money—Thistle is my friend—Thistle is a philanthropist—I will patronize Thistle."

Then I arrayed myself in my best gown, which was an old one with a patch on the elbow; and my "love of a bonnet," which was an old one, and therefore out of date; and my best mantle, which was an old one and somewhat faded from use; and taking my parasol, which was an old one and under hospital treatment—(the handle was broken and tied together with a piece of twine—I broke it defending the innocent. A noble deed! A big dog set upon Jack and bit him, without any cause or provocation whatever, excepting that Jack was much the handsomest dog). Thus equipped I set forth with a light heart and buoyant step. My friend Thistle was president of one of the Savings Institutions of the city, which Savings Institution was instituted, organized, managed, and run, by the said Thistle and his chivalric colleagues, Spiderwort and Tangleweed, for the sole interest, benefit, and emolument of the widow and the fatherless. That is, they were the custodians of the countless millions gathered and saved for them (widows and fatherless) out of the insolvent estates of their dead husbands and fathers, by humane executors, who work by day and by night, without money and without price, simply for the love of labor, and the love of the widow and the fatherless, and as self-sacrificing humanitarians and the tried friends of the defenceless. Then, again, these public-spirited philanthropists are ably aided and abetted by that humane court known throughout the length and breadth of the land as "beautiful *Probate*." A court, as I have already explained, created and sustained by a disinterested public for the *exclusive* benefit of the widow and the fatherless. A magic court wherein little estates are metamorphosed into colossal fortunes in the twinkling of an eye. A court which is a standing reproach to all poor *live* men, because they do not die and enable their wives and children to rise to a higher plane of society and moneyed positions under the guardianship of beautiful Probate protection, and the fatherly care of lawyers, executors, appraisers, auctioneers, etc.

When I arrived at the Terra-Alba Street Bank I found Thistle in close communion, supported on his right by Spiderwort, and Tangleweed on his left. Before him was a table upon which was piled great masses of deeds and mortgages; behind him was a wall, and hanging upon the wall was the head of Thistle, in oil, surrounded by an elaborate gold frame. The instant Thistle caught sight of my card, which was taken in by the courteous cashier on a silver platter with a golden monogram of Thistle upon it, he dismissed his supports by an august wave of the hand, and begged me to be seated. I had followed close upon the heels of the platter. Seeing how very affable and smiling Thistle was, in spite of my old gloves, I thought I would make it an entirely personal matter, and said, in explanation, how that my small income was not commensurate with the needs of my large body; that as soon as the executors, who were laboring like Vulcans at a forge,

THE HEAD OF THISTLE.

turned over the millions coming to me out of my late husband's *insolvent* estate, I could pay the bank the insignificant loan of ten thousand dollars, the amount which I wished to get, and give a hundred per cent. interest for the use of it.

Thereupon Thistle, waxing eloquent, responded in this wise: "My dear Mrs. Stow, it pains me to the quick to inform you that the bank is only loaning on the instalment plan at this moment, and each month you would have to pay one thousand dollars interest and a part of the principal. You are better off without the loan, for if you failed to pay it we should have to foreclose the mortgage at once, for on no account could we jeopardize the moneys of widows and orphans which are deposited in our strong vaults. You are aware, my dear Mrs. Stow, that it is solely for the enrichment and aggrandizement of the widow and the fatherless that savings banks are instituted. All the disinterested officers labor for that, and for that alone. They have no need to add to their worldly possessions; they are financially strong and able to protect the financially weak. I advise you to get something to do—some kind of an agency business, perhaps. The pocket-stove is having a great run, why not run into the interior with it. The commission is generous, undoubtedly. I only mention this as a sort of tide-over, you know, until the "clear-up" comes, when, of course, you will float in butter."

Thistle smiled in the most gallant and insinuating manner imaginable, when he ceased speaking, and taking up his cigar (not Gilroy) he said that I must excuse him, for his time was worth its weight in golden ingots; but that he should be most happy, at all times and in all seasons, to serve me in his modest position, capacity, etc., etc.

From there I slowly wended my way to the Odd Fellows' Savings Bank, and thought it very odd that they had no money to lend. The grave cashier informed me that there was not a sixpenny piece in the bank but *emergency* money. That being a new currency, to me, I requested him to explain its meaning. He replied that nothing of an earthly nature could give him greater pleasure than to enlighten my darkened understanding upon that point. Then he took his pencil from its bracket, at the side of his head, and ran it up and down through the oily fringe over the bracket, and replaced it ere he finished what he had not commenced—a definition of emergency money. Coming back to himself at last, for he seemed to have fallen into a pit of reflection, he continued, or began rather, by saying, "Emergency money, Mrs. Stow, is a stipulated amount which never, under any circumstances, is allowed to be withdrawn from the vault. It could not be removed to create a corner in the stock market, even, so stringent are the rules and regulations. This bank is devoted entirely to the well-being of widows and orphans. You can get all the money you want at the Murphy Bank. They have got more money to loan than all the other saving banks put together."

I expressed my unbounded obligations for the gratuitous information, and was soon inside of the Murphy Bank. Meeting a consequential-looking personage with his hat off, I asked him if I had the honor of addressing President O'Flaherty? "No," he made answer, with a look of amazement that I should mistake any one in such an exalted position. "I am not up to that gentleman's ears. You will find *him* at his desk beyond that door," pointing to a folding-door at the further end of the counter, "laboring for the benefit of widows and orphans. Walk right in, madam, he does not stand upon ceremony." Michael O'Flaherty looked over the top of his spectacles as I entered, but immediately lost all consciousness of my presence, apparently, in the summing up of a long column of figures. I sat down unbidden and bided my time. It soon came, however, and he asked what he could do for me. I explained that I was a widow, and as his bank was created solely for the benefit of this class of unfortunates, I had waited upon him to obtain the loan of a small sum of money—only ten thousand dollars. He was familiar with my property, but said that all the money in the bank was promised for days, weeks, and months in advance, to the patrons of the institution; that it might be weeks, months, years, decades even, before there would be a two-bit piece in the bank to loan to outsiders.

"But *I* am not an outsider," I pleaded, "I am a *widow*." "Yes, I know," he continued, as he carefully folded the paper containing the column of added figures, and putting it into his breast pocket, buttoned his coat tightly over it, "but you are not one of *our* widows, who has deposited her fortune with us. We must serve our own first."

This furnished me with a new idea. I would go to the Mahometan Savings Bank—there I had money on deposit. They could not refuse me there. I felt, as I stepped into this bank, on my native heath. Here I was a part—a very small part, to be sure—of a noble institution; here I should be recognized as a true sheep of the fold; here was a part of my fleece in surplus funds; here I was a fraction of the whole; a millionth of a decimal, perhaps, still that was something. Pausing at the counter, I saw Toombs, the president, in the arena. He came solemnly forward when he recognized me. Toombs never smiles on widows. Toombs is circumspect in all his bank ways. He is never caught prowling about after dark in forbidden places—without a lighted candle in his spiritual lantern. He never visits the *Jardin Mabille* in Paris, nor its like in London or New York, unless he is accompanied by Mrs. Toombs.

I boldly stated my case to him, but I got a gloomy look, and a gloomy reply. "It is quite impossible to accommodate you," he said. "We are calling in money—instead of loaning it out." "But," I exclaimed, taking up the real estate circular, which contained the daily record of mortgage loans, that was lying before me on the counter, "what does this mean? Here are several new loans that were made only yesterday." He did not stop to answer my impertinent question, but escaped into his private den at the rear of the bank.

Going home late—weary and dejected with my unsuccessful efforts, I was met at the threshold of my door, by a happy suggestion. It was this: Write to the Savings Bank Board. Men, collectively, particularly where there is a well-filled sideboard, are often more amiable and obliging than when they are isolated and alone in their unapproachable decisions. Therefore, after partaking of a modest repast, I penned the following appeal:

To the Honorable The Savings Bank Board of the City and County of San Francisco, State of California, United States of North America, Western Hemisphere of the Political Division of the Surface of the Orb Earth, situate in the Great Planetary System of the Universe, 91,430,000 *miles from the Sun, and* 238,833 *miles from its nearest Neighbor the Moon.*

GENTLEMEN—I want the loan of a small amount of money, $10,000, to build two houses, to make two homes for the shelterless wayfarers who come to this balmy coast—and to the balmy breezes of San Francisco, in search of health. I am actuated by purely philanthropic motives—I am, in fact, a philanthropist. Besides, I am a *widow*, which makes a strong claim of itself—in short, a double claim in this direction, for I have been twice a widow—once a woman, and twice a widow. I am a half orphan besides—that strengthens the claim, in fact it makes it two claims and a half. Therefore, I pray your honorable body individually, or collectively, to grant my petition; and my blessing shall descend upon you like golden rain and liquid sunshine.

Your most humble petitioner,
(Signed,) MARIETTA LIZZIE BELL-STOW.

At the first regular meeting, Mr. Killkins, the chairman of the board, read the petition, after which it was ordered to be laid *under* the table. Later, when

Lovely looked the amber rain
In a glass of foin champain,

the petition was ordered to be re-read. It was dragged from its ignoble hiding-place amid uproarious shouts of laughter, and ornamental side-splitting expletives. "Wants money," said Mr. Scumpling, the secretary, after the second hearing. "She might want something more difficult to furnish."

"What could that be?" exclaimed Mr. Judas, the treasurer, as he playfully toyed with his empty glass, poising it first on his forefinger, then on his thumb, and suddenly capsizing it over an imaginary fly, or wasp, or sovereign—then raising his eyes to the ceiling, he struck a pose which rivalled Raphael's Angels.

"A husband," suggested Mr. Thistle, the president, leering over the top of his gold bowed spectacles. "You had better be on your guard, Killkins, or she'll snap you up before you can cry quarter."

Mr. Killkins, with a bashful look, smothered a sneeze in the folds of a cambric handkerchief, which looked as though it had just returned from a long journey.

"Yes," chimed in Mr. Snifter, a small member of the Committee on Home Relations, "widows are dangerous animals to be at large. I'd have every one of them—after they had deposited their money in the savings banks—shut up in a mad-house as incorrigible lunatics."

"Oh, ah! Snifty. You have a vulnerable place in your bachelor-mail, evidently, that has recently been penetrated by a dart, shot from a widow's bow, ha, ha, ha!" Shouted Old Barnacle, the

BI BARNACLE.

blossom of whose nose just showed above the rim of his glass—and, rising, he proposed a health to all submissive widows, who have money in savings banks at a low rate of interest, or whose homes were pledged to those institutions, on money loaned at a high rate of interest.

"Order, gentlemen," shouted President Thistle, swelling with importance. "Shall we let Widow Stow have the money? Yes or no?"

"No!" came from the Board, in harmonious unison. Then they formed themselves into a ring—a bankers' ring—and touching glasses, sang, keeping marvellous time with their hands and feet:

> "High Biddy Martin, tiptoe fine;
> Bankers love money, bankers love wine.
> Bankers are wise men, widows are green;
> They live on skim milk, bankers on cream.
> Bankers are sharpers, widows are ninnies;
> They deal in pennies, bankers in guineas.
> High Biddy Martin, skip toe fine;
> Bankers love widows, bankers love wine."

This song, with an extra glass to wash it down, terminated the "important business meeting." The secretary had been ordered to report the adverse decision of the board to Mrs. Stow, and with a parting "Health to the Board," they separated for the night—and perhaps for a week, unless something of an unusual nature should demand an extra session. Each nose pointed homeward, and each foot, and each pair of feet, obeyed the direction. Double men thought of wives (it is to be hoped) and little ones; single men, of—of sweethearts (possibly), cigars and slippers (no doubt about the latter)— as they struck out in diverging lines. Snifter accompanied his bachelor brother Killkins to the door of his lodgings, but declined to ascend to his skylight parlor, it being somewhat late. Wringing his friend's hand he warned him, in the language of Veller, the elder, with an eloquent gloom in his small gray eyes, that peered out from under a hedge of eyebrows like a ferret's, "to bevare of vidies."

Slowly, thoughtfully, Mr. Killkins ascended the first flight of stairs; the second landing was struck in the same meditative mood; but his movements were perceptibly accelerated in the remaining home stretch. Being in a condition to use his key to unlock the door of his chamber, instead of his jack-knife, he was soon inside of a small room with a small iron bedstead propped up against one side of it, upon which was a small bed and a small pillow, with a not over clean case upon it; a small stove, with a broken door, which served the double purpose of a spittoon and cigar-stump receptacle, stood under the mantelpiece; a small table with a broken mirror hanging on a rusty nail over it, two ricketty chairs and a work-stand completed the garniture of the small room.

"Let's see, let's see!" soliloquized Mr. Killkins, after recovering his breath, cut short off by the effort of mounting four flights of stairs, particularly the last two, and removing the muffler from his long neck. Mr. Killkins was a precautious bachelor, and guarded against the fogs and damps of the bay. "Let's see! Widow Stow has this handsome property on 'Nob Hill' which she wants to mortgage, not exactly on 'Nob Hill' proper, but in full view of it, and she is a fair to middling writer, which talent might be improved by a brilliant side-light." Here Mr. Killkins looked approvingly at the reflection in the broken mirror and smiled, and the reflection in the broken mirror smiled back approvingly upon Mr. Killkins. "If she would consolidate with

KILLKINS IN THE PARK.

a partner of *brains*," he continued, as if addressing the reflection, "the firm might prove a financial success, a *v-e-r-y handsome* financial success. Nothing like getting up in the world" (figuratively) "and only money makes the mare go."

Saying which Mr. Killkins unbuttoned his coat, laid aside his hat and gloves and cautiously seated himself in one of the rheumatic chairs, with one foot on the stove and the other on the table, and fell into a brown study. Starting out of it, and bringing his fist down upon the table with a forcible emphasis, he exclaimed, *a la Bumble*, "I'll do it, I'll do it, *I'll* propose! She'll jump at the chance of seeing herself in print as the *Honorable* Mrs. Killkins, wife of the *ex*-distinguished member of the Lower House, from Red Dog. Yes, I'll do it! She shall not pine in weeds and loneliness any longer. She shall orange blossom into the garden of society. She shall be Mrs. Killkins, the *Honorable* Mrs. Killkins, wife of the Red Dog member.

"She is full of enterprise—and wants! Wants Killkins. She shall have Killkins. Killkins shall be her right bower. She shall name all her air-castles Killkinses, Killkins' Hospital, Killkins' Reformatory, Killkins' Sanitarium, Killkins' School of Design, Killkins' Co-operative Union. She has a diversity of

talents, she may yet turn her attention to medicine—
'*quack*' medicine, and then all the banner-rocks
between here and the Atlantic will herald the marvellous curative qualities of Killkins' court-plaster,
and Red Dog salve; of Killkins' Delirium Tremens
Extractor, and Red Dog Pain Killer; of——" but
here Mr. Killkins was interrupted by a yawn.

Heeding the silent eloquence of his corns, Mr. Killkins removed his boots, by the aid of the superfluous
chair, and shoved his toeless stockings into slippers
down at the heels which had seen much service, but
otherwise were as comfortable as old friends.
Lighting a cigar he took up a copy of *Probate Confiscation*, and looked long and ardently at the stone
picture of the future Mrs. Killkins. As he gazed, he
continued his soliloquy in this wise: "She looks
mild—they say she is high-strung—perhaps she is.
Behind these quiet lips there is a tongue and teeth.
She says she never had the toothache in her life.
She'll need a snaffle-bit, and a tight rein and a firm
hand to control her, 'for discipline must be maintained.' I can do it! I'm as firm as a rock—a rock
of adamant. There'll be but *one* head to the house
of Killkins. She calls the members of my profession
Philistines. She'll find me a *Samson*, instead, whose
strength don't lie in his hair."

As Mr. Killkins said this he passed his hand over his shining poll with a horrible grin of satisfaction. There was not a spear of anything there to pull, shave, or cut. "She's plump," he continued, "not fat, bah! I hate fat, but, like Tom Moore, am somewhat partial to flesh. Wonder if she is partial to bones?" Another smile from the skeleton reflection in the glass greeted his admiring eyes. Killkins was not fat. He was very lean. He had very little muscle to boast of, even, but what he lacked in that direction was made up in bones.

"I must write and propose this very hour. I am full of the subject and must discharge cargo, or I shan't be able to close my eyes to-night," saying which he turned from the captivating apparition in the broken glass, and, closing the book, opened a small drawer in the table and drew forth some delicate French note paper. "Here are my obedient servants, pens, ink, and paper—a lovely rose-tint with cupids in the corner. She'll never suspect that it is *old* paper, purchased years ago to make love to Old Barnacle's Betsey; and that she jilted me and took up with Bi Barnacle. What taste! But to business! It's getting late and growing cold. Ah! my enchantress, Widow Stow! I can exclaim with Misther Sthrong:

'Arrah, none o' yer bordin' schule misses,
  Yer shwate thimid craythurs fur me,
Who rave aboot koopid an' blisses,
  Yit noo not what aythur may be ;
I dcon't fale at arl sinthimintil,
  Fur romanze I cares niver a rap,
But gimme a joolly an' jintle
  Rich widdy in wades an' a cap.'"

MR. KILLKINS' AVOWAL AND PROPOSAL.

HOME, HOUR, *midnight*.

MY ADORABLE MRS. STOW : As Chairman of the Savings Bank Board Committee, I beg to inform you that your appeal to that august body, collectively, was abortive ; but it struck deep, individually, in one responsive heart. I, Mrs. Stow, will loan you the money" (borrowed from the bank at a nominal rate of interest). "individually, in case you accept my offer. I am a bachelor, a lawyer by profession, and an ex-member of the Legislature, lower house, from Red Dog. *Honorable* stands before the name of Killkins and it was honorably obtained. Will you share the glory of that name and the comforts of my home" (prospectively on Nob Hill, or in full view of it) ? "In other words, will you be-*Stow* upon me the felicitous delight of crowning you with the title of Killkins ? It is an old name and an old family" (of bone-boilers and *chiffoniers*). "My father has seen service, honorable service" (beside a soap-vat) "and my mother was born" (in a garret) " on the banks of the Seine. *Will you be mine?*

TRUE SPUNK KILLKINS.

After the offer was under envelope and mucilage, the author of the daring deed still sat with his thoughts roaming in the speculative future. He pictured himself as agent of the renowned Mrs., Honorable Mrs., Killkins, taking in millions of money at lecture halls and on orders for Red Dog salve and Killkins' plaster. Gradually he tilted back in his chair, which canted sidewise against the bed, and was lost, swallowed up, as it were, in a fitful, uneasy slumber. His dreams took up the broken thread of thought and continued the panorama, which rapidly assumed a different coloring. Killkins saw himself as scene-shifter, errand boy, and usher, whom no one noticed, and when a creature with hair enough on his head to upset the universe, if it had belonged to Samson, sent the distinguished lecturess, the Right Honorable Mrs. Killkins a bouquet of pansies and heartsease, and saw himself, in this quaking dream, kicked under a bench when he demanded satisfaction of this hairy individual. He awoke in a cold sweat, with a cold in his head, and a crick in his back, and with a crazy feeling all over, and, I am ashamed to chronicle the weakness of Killkins, but he burnt up the letter and remains single Killkins to this day. A preserved bachelor who feels that he was once nearly unbalanced over the crater of Vesuvius.

After many days' anxious waiting I received a brief note from the secretary of the board, saying that my request was denied. The same evening a friend called to see me, and as I was feeling quite depressed over my failure in not getting the money, and he being greatly distressed on account of my sadness, I was forced to explain my position.

"What did you go to Old Thistle for?" he exclaimed. "Don't you know that his *bank*, as it is called—miscalled—is nothing but a broker's office? *Bank!* why Old Thistle, Spiderwort and Tangleweed carry the whole concern, directors and all, in their breeches pockets. And what have the Odd Fellows and Masons to do with the institutions that sport their names, pray? Nothing at all, my dear madam. They are all run for the benefit of individuals, for the sole benefit of Smudge, Fudge, Budge, as the case may be—for whoever is at the head of them. There is not one of them that will let *you* have the money." "Why not?" I questioned. "My property is surely good security for the sum I wish to borrow." "True! But what is to be gained by letting *you* have the money? Are those men ever guilty of a disinterested act? Never! and I repeat the assertion that Old Thistle, and Old O'Flaherty, and the whole kit and boodle of the sanctimonious, long-headed, swell-heads and block-heads are no better than curb-stone brokers."

I was shocked beyond measure to hear him speak so irreverently of those highfallutin functionaries, that were devoting their time and energies to the wellbeing of widows and orphans, and said as much to him.

"Widows and orphans!" he exclaimed with the greatest disgust. "Is it possible, Mrs. Stow, that a woman of your experience can be bamboozled, excuse the expression, into the belief that the labors of love, of such men, extend beyond themselves and their personal aggrandizement? The only reason in the world that they refused you the money was because they knew perfectly well that they would never be able to sell you out. When they deal directly with widows they want a class that knows nothing about business, and then they—the widows —are easy to handle and fleece. You just look at the advertising columns of the *Bulletin* and see the estates belonging to widows advertised for sale on delinquent mortgages. Who bids in these estates, at half price, under the auctioneer's hammer? Agents for these humane brokers; and this is the *modus operandi* of direct dealings with widows. Those bankers knew it would be impossible to net your property, so you did not get the money."

"But they said they were not lending money, now."

"Humbug! I can go to any one of those banks, to-morrow, and get all the money I want. I can get $15,000 on your property, by dividing the percentage you pay me for getting it with the cashier."

"Is it possible!" I exclaimed, "that our gallant 'protectors' devour us in this manner?" "Possible!" he continued. "If you doubt my word, you just advertise for the money and you will find that any real estate agent can get it at any and all of the savings banks in this city, which have refused you. He won't explain the process, probably, but you will understand it. You want the money, and it is worth while to try this course. Write the advertisement and I will take it down to the *Chronicle* office as I go home."

I did as he advised me to do, and if you care to know the upshot of it you will find it set down in the next chapter.

SCENE THE FOURTH.

"I'VE GOT IT."

Instar canem et lupum.

My advertisement ran thus: "*Wanted the loan of ten thousand dollars on partially improved city property.*" I *was painfully* innocent of the effect of such a public announcement of my impecuniosity, but I soon came to a realizing sense of the somewhat peculiar position it placed me in—in regard to myself and others. Before daylight the next morning the door-bell of the lodging-house on Clover Street, in which I occupied a small but respectable hall bed-room over the front door, began to ring ting a ling, ling, ling, ling, a ting, ting, ting, and the ling and the ting never ceased. Then I heard a squadron of footsteps in the lower hall, and nimble feet mounting the stairs. Mingling with the din of bell and footsteps I could distinguish the sound of *my* name shouted in all accents from the deepest cellar of chest to the highest garret of head. It crescendoed up the stairs and diminuendoed down the stairs; it echoed through the halls, and was caught up in the street. Something dreadful has happened, I thought. Some great calamity has befallen the city. It is on fire, or an earthquake has swallowed it up, or a tidal-wave has drowned it, or Chinatown has risen, or it is crack o' doom. Something's up! The roar in the street and hall becoming louder, I sprang out of bed, slipped into dressing-gown and slippers, and, seizing a match, lighted the gas and threw open my door— just as an army of men, in single file, showed itself above the banisters.

"Are you *Mrs. Stow?*" gasped the mouth of the head, and I could hear the refrain reverberating all the way down the ascending line until it was lost in the distance.

"I am," I made answer, wondering if, like poor Skimpole, I was going to be "*took*" by a regiment of Coavinses, or if I had in any way broken the peace, because I was not a peaceful, patient, quiescent, abnegating widow.

"You want money?" continued the grotesque looking head (red-head) of the advancing column.

"Yes," I replied, "lots of it."

"Yes, ten thousand dollars?"

"Yes."

"I've got it," said he, edging himself into the room uninvited, and sitting down among the blankets on the lounge.

"*I*'ve got it," said the second deliverer, pushing past me, and sitting down on my one chair and in my best bonnet.

"*I*'ve got it," echoed the third, leaning up against the door-casing, quite out of breath. The room was too small to admit of more than two persons besides myself and bed—which was no bed at all, but a lounge. If it had been a bed it would have turned us all out of doors, for it would have taken up all the space—excepting perpendicular space.

"*I*'ve got it," screamed a fourth, clutching at the banisters and mopping his hot face with a soiled bandanna, while his eyes bulged out like bullets as he glared at those who had got the start of him.

"I've got it," came fainter and fainter along the sounding-line like voices in a well.

"First come, first served," I remarked to the head man among the blankets.

"That's right, sounds like business," he replied, complacently stroking his chin, upon which was a rank growth of unkempt stubble. "My name's Gobetween. I got the money of Old Thistle, the president of the Terra Alba Street Bank. He said *you* had been there after it, but that it was so disagreeable transacting business with a *woman*, particularly a strong-minded one, that he would have nothing at all to do with you. But you see *I*'m not so fastidious. I think we can git along tip-top."

"Undoubtedly," said I. "What commission do you charge?"

"Wall, I'll be kinder easy with you seein' you've lost so much by scoundrils, an' seein' you're a widder inter the bargin. I'll ony charge you five per cent."

"I'll do it for three," chimed in number two, moving uneasily in my "bunnit."

"I'll do it for two-narf—narf—nar—na—n——," came up from the well.

"Where did *you* get the money?" I continued, addressing number two, for I was becoming greatly interested in this side game played by the unseen hands of the banks.

"I got it at the Odd Fellows' Bank," he replied. "The cashier told me not to let on as you were there after it."

"But, he declared to me, in the most positive terms, that there was only '*emergency*' money in the bank."

"Well," the lucky man responded, as a gleam of satisfaction crossed his face, "you see we are old friends—*chums*, you know—and he'd oblige me when he wouldn't a stranger."

"*Just so!*" I ejaculated, and there was more in it than those astute "middle men" had dreamed of in their philosophy. Then I addressed myself to the door-casing man, and inquired where he was so fortunate as to secure the money. He hesitated for a moment, and then said: "I got it at the Murphy Bank. Old O'Flaherty advised me to keep shady,

GO-BETWEENS.

but of course you won't blab!" "Of course not!" I made answer, "women never do." Turning to the bullet-eyed successful financier, who had sat down on the top stairs or landing, I repeated the inquiry.

"O, *I* can get money at any of the banks," he said, consequentially, as he twirled his thumbs and turned up his eyes as though, by introversion, he was observing the cunning workings of his own brain.

"It's no consequence *where* I got it, is it? All you want is the money, as I understand it. What's the odds where it comes from so long as you get it? All you've got to do is to pay me my commission, and the interest on the sum loaned, monthly in advance. That's a very simple transaction. No difficulty about it."

At that instant a new voice like a clarion blast swept up the stairway, calling to me in the dulcet notes of my landlady; and these were the notes, which consisted of whole notes, half notes, quarter notes, eighth notes, sixteenth notes, thirty-second notes, and so on—but no rests.

"Misthres Sthow, whativer do ye mane bringin' sich a vile rabile inter a dacint womun's hoose? Git oot, git oot, ye varmints, or I'll brake yer hids wid me brumstic'. Lawks alive! de strate iz shwarmin' wid 'em, an' howiver I'm ter git oot afther me mate fur brakefust de blissed Lard only noze. Saints in glowry dafind us! if here baint wan uv de crazy craythurs in a bull-oon, flyin' throo the air, an' anoother stakin onter de lamp-posht, an' sthill anoother in de ash-barrul. Och! howly Mither! They beez on de sthaple uv de churruch, round de carner, an' on me hoose-top."

"Arrah! Biddy O'Muligan," shot up from the

bowels of the lower regions, "de shmoke is all in de kaychin, an' de fire wunt burrun at all, at all, an' de inyuns baint doon, an' me ize be gist poot oot, intarely, wid de shmoke. I gives yez warnin, Biddy O'Muligan, I laves termorrer. Booty Hoonysookle kant loose her karacther wid de loiks o' yez, in sooch a hoolabulloon place as this."

"Och! de mazarable boozzards have lit on de chimbler-top," screamed Mrs. O' Muligan, with eyes aflame. Her head and arms were bare, and her banged forelock stuck straight up, like the quills on the fretful porcupine, and the tail of her gown was caught up, and thrust in the placket-hole. In this plight she ran down the steps, overturning several small boys and one light-weighted "go-between," and planting herself in the middle of the street, with arms akimbo, shouted, "Come doon, come doon, yez'll sit me hoose on fire ye murtherin blackguards, come doon, I say."

"Mine Got in himmel!" cried little pumpkin-colored Hans Schnider (from his seat on the ridgepole) as he wiped his glowing face and rubbed his short legs, that looked for all the world like a pair of old-fashioned saugage stuffers suffering from an attack of gout. "I's got der monish all in mine pag for Madame Shtow, und I likes ter prake mine pack in dew pieces climin up ter der dop mit it, I puts mine pag on der chimbler, und here I rhestz misel a leedle."

"Git oot, git oot I tell yez. O purlishe, purlishe!" shrieked Mrs. O'Muligan, dashing up and down the front steps in a frenzy of despair. "I shall go stick, stark, raving mad, I know I shall. Git along wid ye! Sooch a rabble of b'y's; the loiks of yeez wuz niver sane in 'Cisco. Coom doon, I tills ye," shaking her fist at Hans.

"Ole ooman," he called from his perch, "be quiet. I's got der monish fur Madame Shtow vat vants ten tousand dollar."

"Misthres Shtow don't live on top uv de hoose, she lives inside uv it—mor's de sorrer to Biddy O'Muligan. If ivir I have anoother *Chrobate* widdy oonder me ruff may I be thared and fithered, an' soused in de bay."

"Ease off yer spankersheet, Biddy," said a bulbous-nosed old salt, as he blew the ashes from his pipe preparatory to refilling it, "or you'll run foul of a snag and spile that purty face o' yourn afore you know it, if you don't."

"Howld yer tung, ye salt-water monster," retorted Mrs. O'Muligan. The admonition was accompanied with a scorching look that would have turned the old

Captain to "cinder," if he had not been so well preserved by brine and tobacco.

"Whar's yer dorg, Schnider?" shouted the mob. I do not cast any reflection upon the middle-men, by calling the impromptu gathering a mob, for they were all, evidently, peaceable, business-loving men. But there is always an idle, mischievous element that capers in and takes part in every street gathering, and it was amply represented on this occasion. "I say, whar's yer dorg?" reiterated the noisy throng, to

HANS SCHNIDER AT HOME.

the accompaniment of catcalls, groans, blowing of Christmas horns and rattling of trombones. "He's left his voice at home to keep Mrs. Shmerekase company, he has, but Biddy O'Muligan's got enough billingsgate for both. She could vake the seven sleepers with that silver tongue of hern, she could, and not half try."

"Shet yer clack," said my landlady, "how dare ye shpake my name in de same brith wid owld Sourkrouts?"

"Who calls Hans Schnider, Sourkrouts? I comes sthrait down, und mit mine fisht I poots von hed on im vat calls me Sourkrouts."

"Come doon, come doon, that's gist what I want," screamed the lady, turning black in the face and quivering with rage. "I've got a shotgun in the kaychin filled to the mizzle fur gist sooch craythurs as ye beez." Changing her tactics, she resorted to tears and pathos, saying: "Oh, that Pathric O'Muligan wuz here to protict his own darlint. I could cry me ize oot, so I cood, fur iver lettin a woomun inther me hoose that makes a mob in de strate."

I waited to hear no more, but addressing the "Go-betweens," who had remained stoically indifferent and immovable during the mêlée, said, "Give me your names, gentlemen, and I will wait upon you at your offices, or communicate with you by letter. My landlady is very much put out, so much so that she cannot get in, I fear, judging from the noise at the door. Therefore, I pray you not to stand upon the order of your going, but go at once." I then stepped out of my window upon the little balcony in front of it and looked down upon the struggling mass in the street, which was filled to overflowing. The overflow surged up streets, alleys, fences, lamp-posts, doorsteps, and telegraph-poles. Seeing it growing suddenly dark (it was now after sunrise) I looked up and discovered that the entire space over the street was entirely filled with balloons. Some of them were nothing but bushel baskets buoyed up by bladders and umbrellas; others, more pretentious, floated respectable sized national banners, with parachutes decorated with small flags bearing the magic device or motto, "I've got it, $10,000." One man, middle-man, hung across the telegraph wire with a balancing pole in one hand, while with the other he frantically flourished a check for $10,000. I was speechless with amazement, until I was hit on my head very forcibly with a small piece of rock attached to a card held by a string. Upon the card was written, in a bold hand, "Mrs. Stow, do you want $10,000? I've got it." Before I recovered from the shock of the blow (which had quite stunned me for the moment, it was thrown with such unerring skill), I heard the fire bells ringing, and, oh, horror of horrors, the alarm was turned on from that ward and that street. I could distinctly hear the engine whistle, and men shouting and swearing (firemen, under such circumstances, are apt to be profane), in the next street. The instant after I was drenched from head to feet by the blinding spray of a stream of water dashed against the house just above my head. Believing the building to be on fire I sprang through the open window so suddenly, supposing the room to be vacant, that I upset three middle-men and one principal, who were sitting on the edge of the wash-stand, ere I reached the closet wherein were stored my trunk and valuables.

Seeing neither fire nor smoke, and coming back to my lost senses, I rightly conjectured that it was a false alarm to clear the streets. I ran back to the window and hastily shut it to keep out the water which was pouring in a flood over the tops of the houses and running in rivers down the street. I watched with no little amusement the downfall of the balloonists; such of them as had not taken timely warning and escaped to dry quarters. One old usurer and pawnbroker was sailing through the air, earthward, on top of his inverted basket, whilst his red, green, and yellow bladders, which had sustained his light weight in mid-air, shot heavenward like sky-rockets. The tails of his claw-hammer gabardine were in the position of a trident; his skullcap was about two inches above and behind his bald head; his eyes seemed fixed and starting from their sockets, so eager was their gaze. He was kneeling on the bottom of the basket, and his whole appearance was strongly suggestive of the infuriated cat upon the cottager's back during morning devotions. Following the direction of his eyes I saw a bag of gold lying in the street, with a ghastly rent in the side of it, through which twenty-dollar pieces were rolling out and gambolling playfully away in perspective, or sportively disappearing altogether in the gutters, or losing themselves in the pockets of the ragged urchins that were not afraid of the wet.

Remembering the man I had seen dangling on the telegraph wire, like an old piece of carpet over a clothes line, I eagerly looked in that direction in search of him. He was still there, but in a dreadful plight. I could see nothing of his check and pole, and his hat was gone. He had evidently served as a target for every stream of water played, for he was as damp and miserable-looking as the nine beautiful and accomplished young men were that Mr. Dickens mentions in an after-dinner speech. Those nine beautiful and accomplished young men gallantly plunged into the deep blue sea, risking their nine lives to rescue one beautiful and accomplished young lady, who had plunged into the blue sea before them, in order to test the love of *ten* beautiful and accomplished young men, all of whom the beautiful and accomplished young lady was more or less in love with; and all of whom wanted to marry her. But when the beautiful and accomplished young lady stood safely upon deck, surrounded by her nine dripping admirers, she could not decide which she loved best, because they were all *wet*. Thereupon the thoughtful captain advised her to take the *dry* one, which she did, and they lived happily ever afterward: so sayeth the record.

Before I had time to speculate further upon my moist, would-be servitor, the hook and ladder company came along and took him down from his perilous position.

Bidding a rap on my door "come in," I was confronted by my amiable landlady. She presented the same appearance that she had in the street, with this exception—she, like myself, was drenched with water. I requested her to be seated. "No!" she exclaimed most emphatically, "I haint coom to make a frindly call, not by a long chalk, but ter till yeez ter be afther lavin here; an' de sooner de bither."

"I am very sorry, Mrs. O'Muligan, for the discomfort you have experienced on my account this morning," I said very meekly, "but it shall not happen again, believe me. You have been so very kind to me when I have been sick, comforted me with toast and tea, and such little attentions, that I am doubly aggrieved over this mishap. I do not expect to find such disinterestedness everywhere I go. It is very unusual, judging from my limited experience in lodging-houses; therefore I say again, I am very sorry."

"Misthres Sthow, ye needent think to mollify me wid yez foin spaches; I'm none uv yer doughheded softies that yeez con blarney wid soft soap an' blind wid the lather on't. So I sez go! afore Pat cooms home to find falt and jaw."

"Mrs. O'Muligan, it is not convenient for me to move just now," I continued, "and if you will allow me to remain I will give you five dollars extra on my room rent this month, and I will make it all right with "Beauty" (the maid-of-all-work, who had given "warnin") besides; she will stay if you ask her to. It was very stupid in little Hans Schnider to put his money bag on the chimney and stop the draft; but I am not to blame for that, and therefore should not suffer on account of it. He is gone now, and is not likely to return after such a ducking as he got from the hose-men." Seeing that Mrs. O'Muligan was still unable to decide the question, " stay or not stay," I laid a five-dollar gold piece on the bureau beside which she was standing, and taking a bottle in which I kept drinking-water (nothing stronger), went to the bath-room to fill it. When I returned I found, to my relief, that the money and lady had disappeared together.

Exchanging my wet clothes for dry ones, I made a cup of tea on my spirit-lamp, and getting out my commissary department, which was a twelve quart tin pail, I broke my long fast, and cogitated on the curious phases of life, particularly such as overtake Probate widows under "chivalric protection."

My reverie was cut short by hearing—

"Extra, extra," shouted from the street, "here's yer exthra, all about the horrible murther." "What murder?" said a stentorian voice under my window.

"A Mrs. Stow has killed a man," answered the news-vender. "Have an extra, sir, it tells all about how she killed 'im."

"You don't say so," continued the questioner in a still louder key. "I allus thought she'd dew somethin' dreadful yit, ever since she wrote that book. She's crazyer'n bedlum! Who'd she kill? Judge Myrick, or some of the lawyers, or one or both of the executors?"

"She hain't killed nobody ner nuffin," sings out another extra-boy, crossing the street with his arms full of smoking papers. "Somebuddy or sumfin' has killed her, or else she 'n some other man has killed some other feller. Tenerate somethin' or somebuddy's deder'n a door-nail. Have an extra, Old Blunderbuss?"

"No!" said the loud-voiced individual, "I ain't interested in murders."

A boy on the opposite side of the street, with a second edition of red-hot extras, cried out: "'Taint no man murthered. It's she herself that's done for. A woman by the name of Sthow was found before daylight this mornin' in the bay, with her head off. They are draggin' the bay fur the head now."

"Who killed her?" said a dozen voices at once.

"How do I know? I sells the papers what tells yeez all about it. B'y an exthra, ony ten cents an' it gives all de 'ticlers."

I ran into the hall and looking over the banisters saw Beauty standing in the street door with her eyes, ears, and mouth pulled open to their utmost capacity. Calling to her, I threw down a half-dollar and told her to run for her life and get me an extra, and not to let the grass grow under her feet, for they were going off like hot cakes on a frosty morning. I wanted to see how they—the newspapers—had killed me (newsboys can never be wholly relied upon); whether I had fought a duel with small swords or with pistols, shotguns, cannons, or pop-

BEAUTY HONEYSUCKLE.

guns, at long range, short range, or no range at all; whether I had been punctured with a dagger, bodkin, ramrod, foil, carving knife, javelin, skewer, rapier, bradawl, malice, slander or any other deadly weapon with a point to it; whether I was ground to bits in a slow mill or pulverized in an apothecary's mortar; whether I was hit by a hammer, sand-club, beetle, or kicked to death by butterflies; whether I was drowned in the ocean, bay, Mission Creek, Spring Valley reservoir, water-trough, bath-tub, wash-bowl, artesian well or teapot; whether I had been burnt at the stake, or been touched off with a lucifer match, or a match of any sort; whether I had been blown up by a steamboat explosion, or gunpowder, dynamite, crude petroleum, nitro-glycerine, naphtha, or my landlady—I was again cut short in my speculations by the arrival of Beauty, all out of breath, with four extras, which she declared were wet as sop.

The heading of the extra ran thus:

A GREAT MYSTERY! PROBABLY A COLD-BLOODED MURDER HAS BEEN PERPETRATED IN OUR MIDST!!!!!

At an early hour this morning, in fact, on the first trip of the return ferry-boat from San Francisco to Oakland, a man was observed grasping a carpet bag, and greatly agitated. The porter of the boat, a humane gentleman of color, asked him the cause of his anxiety. He—the excited man—said that Mrs. J. W. Stow had advertised that morning for a loan of $10,000, and that he had got the money with him in the bag, and was apprehensive that he might not be the first there, and in that event he should lose his time, which was of priceless value, and also, the expense of crossing and recrossing the bay; that he was an Oaklander, not born there—but that he had adopted the city, or else the city had adopted him. Upon this point, the porter's narrative got tangled. However, he— the porter—offered the stranger some words of consolation and comfort, and retired to his brush and duster. After the passengers had all left the boat, the porter found the bag with its bowels slit open, and the money gone. Therefore, it is conjectured that the poor broker is at this moment furnishing an early breakfast for the infant salmon, at the bottom of the bay—while the thief and murderer is at large. There were only three passengers on the boat, so the assassin had ample opportunity to slay his innocent, confiding victim, and to throw the body, which was a light one, overboard. The entire police force are scenting the track of the murderer, and working up the case. Every city in the United States and Canada, Great Britain and the Continent, China and South America, and the Feejee Islands—are informed by telegraph of all the facts in the blood-curdling, hair-splitting, flesh-creeping, bone-shaking atrocity. After this, no man's life is safe, and we advise all men to take the precaution hereafter to wear their bags and pockets wrongside out, in order to convince thieves and cutthroats that they, the owners of bags and pockets, have no money on their persons. There can be little doubt but that the double-dyed villain will be caught within the next twenty-four hours, for his Excellency, Governor Erwin, has offered $100,000,000 reward for his apprehension, and his *Honor*, Mayor Bryant, has offered a like sum, in the name of the City Fathers of San Francisco, and George Washington, the father of his country. More anon, as the case is worked up.—CHRONICLE OFFICE, 10 A.M.

The same day, at a second and a quarter past four o'clock P.M., this placard appeared upon the *Evening Bulletin* board :

A DIABOLICAL IMPOSITION ! ! !

The "extra" issued this morning by the *Chronicle*, was an unmitigated *hoax*. The man with a carpet-bag on the early

CITY FATHERS.

boat was one of the *locals* on the staff of that eccentric paper, who had been on the scent of a much-desired murder in Oakland—but had failed to discover any. Seeing the advertisement, a bold thought rose in his fertile brain, he would manufacture a murder out of an old carpet-bag, and some waste paper, with which he stuffed it. Thus equipped he played upon the tender sensibilities of the porter, in the manner described in the "extra," and just as the boat touched the wharf, slit up the bag, and casting the waste paper to the four winds, leaped ashore, leaving the ruptured bag to tell its own story. *Behold the result!*

The city of San Francisco has sued Charles de Young for a billion dollars libel, and the great army of citizens who took part in dragging the bay, have torn down the *Chronicle* office, from turret to foundation-stone, and from foundation-stone to turret, and cast the lying press into the bay; at which the bay turned up its nose in unfeigned disgust, and with its undertow, kicked it—the lying press, out into the mouth of the Golden Gate, where it pertinaciously stuck, and in consequence thereof the overflow of the sea is causing the bay to rise at the rate of sixteen feet per minute, and all the inhabitants of the city are seeking safety and dry quarters on Mount Telegraph. They have lynched the rascally local, but the audacious Charles is at large, having given a quintillion bond. *He is safe!* for the trial will not be likely to come off for the next fifty years, and when it does it will be carried up, and up—so that when the punishment comes, as it is sure to come, it will fine and imprison one of Charles de Young's great, great grandsons. This is the meaning of the text, " I will visit the sins of the fathers upon the third and fourth generation."

But the city did not drown, and the local did not die, and the *Chronicle* blossomed forth the next morning as usual; but the how, and the where it was printed, remains a mystery, "past findin' out," to this day.

SCENE THE FIFTH.

AN OPEN LETTER TO THE CHAMBER OF COMMERCE.

Oculis clausis agere.

To the Honorable Members of the Chamber of Commerce, in General Assembly convened:

GENTLEMEN—As many of you are aware that I have not, *as yet*, come into possession of the untold millions which I shall receive at the hands of the able, upright, efficient and swift-footed executors, as soon as they terminate their Herculean labors and are ready to distribute estate; therefore, it will not surprise you perhaps, if I inform you that I am at the present moment—that is, just now, in great need of a small, a *very* small amount of money—two thousand dollars. A mere bagatelle, to be sure, but if I do not get it immediately, I fear—I do not speak positively—I fear, gentlemen, that I may lose all I possess of this world's goods and chattels. My separate property is valued at twenty-five thousand dollars, and I think—I may be in error, however, but I think—it is worth an effort to save it from the auctioneer's playful hammer.

My immediate embarrassment arises out of the playful complications and jocose management of the Gilroy Consolidated Tobacco Company. Every few months they have levied an assessment of ten dollars per share on the capital stock, and as I own a hundred shares, each time the facetious game has been played, by the rubber hands, it has phlebotomized me to the tune of a thousand dollars. Understand me, gentlemen, this is done out of love and good-will towards all concerned, and I in particular. They are greatly exercised in mind, fearing I may die of financial plethora, or luxurious repose and peace of mind. They are a band of brothers — a noble band of brothers. They are the natural guardians of the effects of widows and orphans. Two of the members are the able and upright executors of my late husband's will. They were all, ere his death, his bosom friends and co-laborers in the marts of trade. They would lay down their lives singly or collectively to serve his widow. Ah! such men as they are! My weak hand is impotent to depict their worth; their fair-mindedness; their labors of unrequited love; their heroic deeds—in the management of dead men's estates and the financial care of their widows and orphans.

Pardon the digression, gentlemen! When I touch upon this all-absorbing subject, I am carried out of myself, as it were. My enthusiasm knows no bounds; my love has no limit; my admiration no end; my hopes no fathom. My expectations are unprecedented, unchangeable, undying, eternal. In the light of their deeds I live and move and have my being. But just now, gentlemen, I am impecunious, and I make my situation known to you as friends of the late J. W. Stow, who was once your beloved vice-president. I call upon you as city fathers; as the friends of widows; or, as I might more appropriately put it, as the combined body-guard of all widows, great or small, rich or poor, fat or lean, high or low, handsome or unhandsome, old or young, talented or untalented, accomplished, or unaccomplished; black-headed, brown-headed, red-headed, grizzly-headed, tawny-headed, or hot-headed.

Remember, I came among you years agone, a younger and, consequently, a more captivating widow than I am now, and gave individually—stranger that I was—a thousand dollars, and two months valuable time to one of your most worthy eleemosynary institutions. That act, gentlemen, should prove bread cast upon the waters in this my hour of need. San Franciscans never forget benefits bestowed. Their memory is sublime. Believing this appeal will touch a sympathetic chord in your heart of hearts,

I am, gentlemen, most truly yours,

In beautiful Probate,

MARIETTA L. B. STOW.

Why did I write an open letter to the Chamber of Commerce? Why? Because I did not wish to show partiality. I knew that the members were never all there at any single sitting. That would be an impossibility, for some must, in the usual course of events, be sick, getting married, or otherwise profitably employed, and, therefore, not able to attend. But the great public medium—the medium "*Daily*" penetrates everywhere, even to the bridal-chamber and the invalid's pillow. It is grasped like the hand of an old friend, in the reading-rooms of distant lands. Every one, I argued, that reads my letter, who knew my husband or who knows me, will want to become my benefactor, and what a delight it will be to receive all these charming tokens of remembrance. How they will put to the blush *forever* the cold, cynical sayings, " Out of sight, out of mind ; " " Under the sod all obligations cease," etc. A man may sportively say, as a vivid contrast to his true feelings, and as a sort of mental gymnastics : " True, he, my dead friend, put me in the way to make all the fortune I have, by loaning me money and by gratuitous assistance and advice, when no one else cared whether I begged or starved. But what of that ? I do not need help now. And as to his widow—pooh ! There's no fear of her ever going hungry."

When I had finished my letter, I took it down to the *Chronicle* office. The polite local informed me that it would be necessary to see the proprietor in person, as it was a personal letter, and that he would not be in before ten o'clock.

At that hour—I had remained at the office—I was shown into Mr. de Young's private sanctum. The gentleman was not a stranger to me, and glancing from under his green blind he requested me to be seated, with all the chivalrous gallantry which characterizes the entire staff of the San Francisco *Daily Chronicle*. He then begged my indulgence while he put a short head on a long leader.

While I waited I looked about the little parallelogram of an office with considerable curiosity. "Just the place," I thought, "for sharp ideas to shoot at brain-targets." The room was very cheery. A gay carpet covered the floor, and unique pictures adorned the walls. Some in frames, but more without. There was one of the latter which graphically delineated a street and balcony scene at the time of the great earthquake in San Francisco in '65. In the foreground of this picture stood a man in primitive costume, while another, in a single garment, was gracefully sailing out of the third story window of a fourth story building; a woman was holding an inverted baby, just from the bath, by one foot, while Brambrilla, the sweet singer, appeared in the character of a ghost, clad in a sheet, and nothing more. The houses were all bowing and scraping to each other like fashionable acquaintances, while men, women, and children, in all costumes and no costumes at all, were hobnobbing with sidewalks, lamp-posts, and the cobblestone pavement of the street, and with each other. There were other curious and amusing pictures, with numerous mottoes (emblematic of the taste of the presiding genius) interspersed here and there, like savory side-dishes at a feast. A bust of Hercules stood upon the mantel, and beside it, in a Venetian vase, was a nosegay of rare flowers which scented the whole office. A human skull, that served the purpose of a cigar-stump and ash-tray receptacle, was lying upon the table, whilst under it a lion rampant with a hole in its back did service as a spittoon. Mr. de Young was the centre target. He sat at a little green baize table, or rather, at a table whose top was covered with that legal complexioned fabric. Before him was an inkstand of Genevese workmanship (fashioned after a decapitated bear), and the human skull, which might have belonged to a quillman in its day and generation.

The dazzling droplight was covered by a shade upon which was depicted plump cupids and airy psyches, ever aiming their seen and unseen darts at the handsome target, but ever failing to hit the centre. Upon the white forehead of the invulnerable mark sat another shade, or screen, or blind, which resembled an inverted green crown or wicker basket covered with fig-leaves. I do not mean by this that the covering of the screen was made out of the succulent leaves of the mulberry in their natural state—not at all, because they had gone through many processes of assimulation and change; they had nourished the worm, and from this nourishment the worm had been enabled to spin the cocoon, and from the cocoon the shining silk was reeled, twisted, colored, warped, woofed, webbed, sold, purchased, cunningly cut and fashioned, and made up as a covering for that wire-cage of a screen, which protected the dark orbs of the midnight toiler from the too ardent gaze of the penetrating gas—a gas so pure and brilliant that a ten hundred thousand million candle-power would be as a rush-light beside it. I marvel that Mr. de Young has not become stone blind long ere this, in spite of his two screens, from the effects of it. I would advise him, as a precautionary measure, and to avert any such dire calamity, to put away his psyches and cupids, and green silk, and green baize, and to cover his gas with a blue plate-glass shade an inch and a quarter thick, and his eye-cage with blue silk, and his table with blue baize, and take up the gay carpet, with its cornucopias, roses, shamrocks, and mistletoe-boughs, and put down a blue carpet, with a blue centre, and a blue border, and have the walls and ceiling of the office, and the bust of Hercules and the lion rampant, and the skull, tinted blue; and the foreground of the earthquake picture touched up with cerulean. I would further advise him to wear a blue coat, and a blue hat, and blue slippers, and a blue dicky, and blue gloves, and wipe his nose on a blue handkerchief, and carry a blue umbrella, and have all the " *Chronicle* men " painted blue, and print the " Daily Morning " on blue paper.

THE MIDNIGHT TOILER.

When I explained to Mr. de Young the object of my visit, and showed him my letter, he said: "If I were you, Mrs. Stow, I would not publish it. Any one of those to whom it is addressed collectively will accommodate you individually. It will cost you six dollars to address them through the vehicle of the press and nothing privately." I thanked him for his kind and sensible advise, but declined to act upon it by promptly paying the six dollars. Then I went home and slept the sleep of the brave.

I was awakened some time during the night, as I supposed, for it was still dark in my room, by a sense of suffocation. I turned over and lighted the gas, which, to my amazement, burned very feebly. The beauty of a small room is this, that like a French kitchen, or steamboat kitchen, you can stand, sit, or lie in the centre of it and reach everything in it. In this respect a small room is a gem of convenience. I looked at my watch and found that it was half-past eight o'clock. What could it mean? There was not a sound to be heard in the street nor in the house. I reached over the other side and pulled up the window curtain. What was that lying up against the open lattice of the closed shutters? It looked like white paper. Could it be snow? Impossible! It never snows in San Francisco. I took my thumb and forefinger, and thrusting them through the lattice, pulled in, not a plum, but one, two, three, half-a-dozen letters addressed to Mrs. J. W. Stow, with "*In haste*" written conspicuously in the corner of each envelope. Tearing open one which bore the imprint of the great seal of the Chamber of Commerce of San Francisco, I read:

Mrs. J. W. Stow:

Dear Madam—The Chamber is ready to appropriate a million of money to alleviate your immediate necessities, if you require it. Your happiness is our happiness; your necessities are our necessities; your peace of mind is our peace of mind. Every heart in this fraternity is skewered and trussed with yours in sympathy. We remember our late brother, and we remember our late brother's widow. We act as one man. Be not surprised at receiving frequent and manifold expressions of our anxiety to comfort, and ability to aid you during the day, for your communication has stirred us like a great horn spoon—if an earthly simile can express the intensity of our feelings.

Yours, till death do us part.

It was signed by the president, five vices, and five hundred members in good standing.

I was so oppressed by the weight of joy and suffocation at the moment I concluded the reading of the ecstatic missive, that I found it necessary to investigate the cause of the limited supply of air. I was apprehensive that something might be out of kilter in the running gear of the planetary system. Perhaps the earth, in an unguarded moment, had caught up with the sun, or the sun had overtaken the earth, or that Saturn had slipped his belts, or that Berenice had slipped off her "back hair," or that some one or all of the celestial dragons had got loose, or that Ursa Major had pitched into Ursa Minor—might not right! I pushed back the lounge, which took the place of a bolt at night, and opened the door, but there did not seem to be a mouthful of air in the gloomy hall. I then tried, with all my might, to force open the outside blinds to the window. I partially succeeded in this when a perfect hailstorm of letters fell about my head and poured in a steady stream over the tops of the blinds, which I could not close again. I was very soon driven out into the hall, for the letters came in so rapidly that I knew that it would only take a few moments to pack the room. I took care, as I came out, to close the door after me, so that the hall would not be flooded too.

I then commenced an investigation, although I could scarcely walk. First I went down to Mrs. O'Muligun's room, and receiving no answer to my repeated knocking, I walked into the dimly-lighted apartment unbidden. My landlady was just taking her head out of the grate, and such a conditioned head as it was, covered with soot and ashes! The banged forelock resembled the stub-end of an enraged scrub-broom. She looked at me and moved her lips, but I could not hear a sound. What did it mean? I spoke to her, and still there was no sound. I could not hear my own voice. I then went up to the second floor front—to Mr. Dumpty's room. Mr. Dumpty knew everything. He was a little roly-poly bachelor, that knew better how to take care of Dumpty than any woman could. Mr. Dumpty was a bald-headed bachelor, who wore glasses and an easy coat, and an easy "westcut," and an easy cravat with flowing ends; Mr. Dumpty also wore easy shoes in the street, and easy slippers in the house; he sat in an easy chair, and had an easy rest for the accommodation of his rheumatic leg—which rest was cushioned with a bit of carpet stuffed with hops on account of their sedative qualities.

Judge of my astonishment at finding Mr. Dumpty in the same humble posture in which I had left Mrs. O'Muligun a moment before. He was kneeling upon the hearth with his little round billiard-ball head thrust clear out of sight up chimney. When I saw the little decapitated body in the easy-coat in that uneasy and unusual position, I shrieked out, at the top of my voice: "Mr. Dumpty, what *is* the matter? Is your head off, or are you hung by the neck in the chimney?" But my voice made not a particle of sound, and going over to the fireplace I pulled poor Dumpty by the coat-tail with such force that his head flew out as suddenly as a cork out of a champagne bottle.

"O Dumpty! what a head!" I exclaimed, when I saw the plight it was in. It was covered with soot. There was soot on the shining crown; soot in the sparse furze that bristled at its base; soot in his ears; soot in his mouth and soot in his eyes, which looked beseechingly at me for a moment and then crept back up chimney, head and all, in company with the gasping mouth and sooty ears.

I realized now, for the first time, what had happened. The house was buried in letters, walled up to the eaves, undoubtedly, thus excluding all the air, excepting what came down chimney; and as every grate had a head in it, there could none escape into the rooms. This state of things had turned the whole house into an exhaustive receiver, and all the heads in the house up chimney. Then I wondered how long I should live, as I had no grate to put my head in, and wondered if I were to fall down on Mr. Dumpty if it would hurt him any. I remember in the experiments made with the feather and bullet, in a glass tube exhaustive receiver, which I had witnessed at school, that when the feather fell on the bullet it did not seem to injure the bullet any.

I began to feel very faint, and sank down upon a

chair. I thought of Mr. de Young's prophetic warning, and if I was ready to die. My *will* was made, there was great consolation in that. I longed to hear a sound, and I struck the marble-topped table with all my remaining strength, but I felt nothing and heard nothing. Then I resigned myself to fate and awaited death, wondering if he would appear in visible form with his somewhat antiquated reaping machine, and which he would be likely to take first, Dumpty or I.

What was that? Oh, joy! a sound, a welcome sound. It was very faint, like the distant chiming of bells. An earthquake would have been hailed with rapture if it had broken the horrible stillness but for a second. "It is a bell," I cried, starting up out of the chair, only to fall down upon the floor; "they are surely carting away the dreadful letters. I will never do another rash act so long as I live, if I get out of this alive, *never!*"

The blessed sounds increased, nearer and nearer they came, until I heard a great slide, like the snow falling from a roof, or a small avalanche, and oh, heaven be praised! Daylight looked slyly in, accompanied by a little air. I raised my eyes in thankfulness at the timely deliverance, and saw Beauty Honeysuckle standing before me. Poor

Beauty! She was anything but beautiful at her best condition; but now she presented a sorry sight. There was blood as well as soot and ashes upon her face and hands. I gave her my hand, and she assisted me to my feet, and going to the window I threw it open, flooding the room with air and sunshine. Then, with the assistance of Beauty, I dragged Mr. Dumpty out of his dark retreat the second time. Finding that there was more air in the room than up the flue, he made no attempt to return to the confined and sooty quarters. The moment he recovered his breath he exclaimed:

"What the *deevil's* to pay? If there hadn't been a grate in my room, I should have been as dead as a pickled herring, long ago." "It's all right now, Mr. Dumpty," I made answer, and beat a hasty retreat to my own room, to avoid further questioning, taking Beauty with me. I then said to her:

"Go into the bath-room and wash your hands and face, and then come and help me pack my things." This was speedily accomplished, and when I gave her some money, in part compensation for what she had suffered on my account, I inquired: "How did you get scratched and bruised so, Beauty? The skin is all rubbed off the end of your nose and the tips of your ears." She replied:

"All uv a sudin I couldn't kitch me brith, an' I jumps oot uv bed onter de floor, an' runs inter de kaychin an' gist krapes oop der chimbler hole, thinkin' 'Cisco had sunk wid a quake. But me hed sthook fast, loik it woz in a vice, an' it woz as mooch as iver I cud do ter git it loose and krape back agin. Howly Mither! Misthiss Sthow, me ize an' mouth, an' nooze wuz chock fool uv soot an' ashes. I niver sore de loikes, no niver since I lift owld Ereland."

"Well, never mind," said I soothingly, "I want you to go now and get me an express wagon, for I must leave this place before Mrs. O'Muligun comes to herself. My rent is paid for two weeks longer. That ought to compensate her for this mishap." I was soon settled in new lodgings, a wiser if not a better woman.

The effect of all this sympathetic correspondence was somewhat remarkable, to say the least, on the general public, but more especially upon the participants who took an active part in it, either directly or indirectly, voluntarily, or involuntarily. It was a memorable day at the Chamber of Commerce, for no sooner had its members dispatched a letter than some new thought or expression of sympathy arose in their minds and they were forced to follow the last tender missive with another and another, and still another, and so on and on, until paper rose in the market, owing to the run on that particular merchandise, to fabulous prices. Five dollars were paid for a single sheet of foolscap (they scorned to use anything smaller), and a corresponding price for envelopes. All the paper dealers went raving mad over their enormous profits, and were sent in a body up to Stockton. Every carrier in the post-office department had his feet entirely worn off and went stumping round on pins, to the horror of the boot and shoe trade. Every member of the Chamber of Commerce that was not travelling in Europe or Japan, or newly married, had to carry their right arms in slings and their heads in wet towels and ice-baskets for months. It took the entire force of cartmen and sixteen thousand steam paddies to cart off the unopened and unread letters and dump them in the bay.

That evening, as the four o'clock ferry-boat was making its usual trip from San Francisco to Oakland, it went aground—or a-*letter*, rather, on a mound of them that an eddy had piled up just off the southern coast of Goat Island. The boat stranded within twenty rods of the pier, and no coaxing would make her budge an inch. In vain the captain gave orders; in vain the engineer rang the bell and blew his whistle; in vain the wheelman tugged at the spokes; in vain the platform men cursed and swore; in vain the porter brandished his scrub-brush and swab; in vain the second edition *Bulletin* boys gnashed their teeth; in vain the one-legged candy man frothed at the mouth; the condition of things grew more perilous every instant.

The boat steadily and majestically rose in air. The tide was coming in; with it came millions of letters with their seals unbroken—for each would-be benefactor had stamped his sympathetic missive either with the great seal of the Chamber of Commerce or his private seal, and San Francisco's sealing-wax is impervious to salt water, and you could circumnavigate the globe in a boat made out of San Francisco envelopes. The situation was appalling. Men grew desperate; they divested themselves of their small clothes, and attaching them to their canes unfurled them to the breeze, as signals of distress; they blew concerted blasts with their noses; fired their concealed weapons into the upper regions; shouted fire at the tops of their voices; women screamed, and babies fainted; little dogs stood first on their heads and then on the tips of their tails; minute-guns were fired incessantly; the whole heavens were lurid with the light of rockets let off from the boat, and still she went up.

The vessel, with its distressed freight, was at least ten feet above water, high and dry upon paper. Soon the entire fleet of the bay was in motion. Ships of war and peaceful merchantmen, steamboats, sloops, brigs, pluggers, yachts, smacks, scows, lighters, gigs, tugs, row-boats, canoes, dugouts, and every and all other crafts known in nautical parlance, bore down upon the benevolent letter-logged boat and crew.

The Oakland pier was covered with the weeping wives and sweethearts of the ascending husbands, and lovers and other enforced prisoners. A curious looking fleet was seen in the distance, putting off from the Oakland shore. It consisted of wash-tubs, bath-tubs, bread-troughs, dish-pans and every other floating household utensil that was large enough to hold an adult person. These impromptu boats were rowed, paddled, and sculled with pudding-sticks, butter-spatters, spades and boot-jacks, in the hands of the wives and sweethearts of such of the ferry-boat's crew as could not spare the time to meet their beloveds on the pier; and as there were no ships or vessels on the Oakland side of the bay, these ladies were obliged to provide their own salt-water conveyances, and they proved themselves equal to the emergency.

It would have moved the heart of a stone to have

heard the lamentations and self-upbraidings of the wives upon the wharf, and the wives in the wash-tub-fleet. One of the latter burst out between her sobs, with, "Dearest Robert had hard-boiled eggs and muddy coffee for his breakfast, and when he casually mentioned it in his most affable manner, I was hasty and said, 'Shet yer hed, Bob Splinter, you're always fault-finding at meals, and growling like a dog with a sore head. Gracious goodness! Its better'n ye deserve.' Oh, I could cry my eyes out, he *is* such a good husband! Boo, hoo, hoo——e!"

A lawyer's wife, standing on the wharf, whose "subjugator" has a looking-glass in his private office, let into his panel, with a green border around it—no, let into the door of his panel—no, let into the panel of his door, I should say—wept a *flood* of tears, saying, "O Noah, sweet Noah, charming Noah, my jewel of politeness, when you swore at the missing buttons this morning, what did I say? Oh, what *did* I say? I said, 'Noah Highwater, aren't you ashamed of yourself? What kind of a bringing-up did you have, I should like to know? Don't you expect an earthquake will open and swallow you up for such conduct? I do, and serve you right, too!' O dear, dear, dear, Noah Highwater!" But I cannot chronicle a millionth part of the expressions of endearment, tears, and anguish of heart which was poured forth in a lavish expenditure upon the merit and endearing qualities of the quaking flesh and blood suspended in mid air that memorable afternoon. It would take gallons of ink, reams of paper, and tons of steel pens and muscle to do the subject justice.

All of a sudden there was a lull, of a minute and a half, in the varied tempest of sounds. The whistle ceased blowing; the bell ceased ringing; husbands stopped swearing, and wives stopped sobbing; all the multitudinous crafts and craftsmen and craftswomen that went to make up the fleet stood still, and the waves stopped flowing and commenced to ebb. Then the boat began to settle, settle, settle, slowly at first, then faster, for the receding waves—the compassionate waves—bore back the letters upon their bosoms in a loving embrace. As the boat struck water, every man furled his flag of distress and lighted a cigar, every woman wiped her eyes and smiled in pleasurable anticipation. The engine began to work, the wheels, cogs, and pistons lent their willing assistance; the boat started, stirred, moved, and when she touched the wharf the heavens—or fog-drifts, rather —were rent in twain by a shout of joy. I shall ring down the curtain here and leave tender imagination to finish the scene upon the pier.

"But how was it possible," you ask, "for all this to have happened in one day?" "Very pertinent to the subject," I reply. "There was an extra session of the Chamber of Commerce at midnight (a cautious secret session; no one but themselves knew its import), to which no outsider, excepting the "*Chronicle* man," was admitted. Mr. de Young appreciating the necessity of prompt, efficient action on behalf of my letter, and rightly conjecturing that there would be a great demand for the issue that contained it, had a hundred millions,

THE CHRONICLE MAN.

over and above his daily circulation of five hundred millions and some odd thousands, struck off, so as to be able to meet the anticipated unusual and unprecedented demand. Just two seconds and a quarter after the minute hand of the great dial of the Chamber of Commerce had assumed the perpendicular, a *Chronicle* man appeared upon the Chamber scene with a thousand of the "first editions" smoking hot from the press.

This is the entire explanation in a nutshell, and I express my unshaken belief, boldly and without mincing the matter, that every fair-minded reader will accept it as such.

SCENE THE SIXTH.

LITTING IN THE CAVE.

From the exciting scenes on Clover Street I went to live in the Cave on the Terrace. There are many terraces in San Francisco, but this was a *particular* terrace on Rosin Street. Opposite was a red wood "mansion," which belonged to a "fat" Philistine whom I had had occasion to know—at a distance— remarkably well. Here, in the above-named mansion, the "fat" Philistine lived, dwelt, and abided with his wife, his two sons, also Philistines, and his two sons' wives; his maid-servants, his man-servants, his dogs, his cats, his birds and whatever other animate or inanimate thing that went to make up his household. The grounds around the "fat" Philistine's mansion were laid out with an eye to taste and somewhat gauged the opulence of the owner. Rare blossoms showed their heads above the yellow-eyed and blue-eyed porcelain barrels that, like two corpulent burghers, guarded the entrance on either side of the stone steps leading up to the outer portal of the red wood "mansion." Fuschias, clyanthuses and roses festooned the walls; knots of pansies, drifts of daisies, and beds of floral beauties, with an ample fringe of greensward, formed a lovely *parterre* which I was never weary of admiring. I think it was kept in such choice order for my especial benefit—*perhaps?* We can never tell exactly in what channel people's benevolence runs, particularly when that benevolence runs so deep that it can neither be seen nor heard, but only felt. However, I both saw and felt in this case, as I often crossed the street on my way down town to gratify my sense of smell as well—all for nothing.

The front of the cave, and the house a-top of it, reminded me of an Italian palace—just such a rambling, pillared contrivance of a dwelling place, warily cropping out of the hill, or more properly, the mountain behind it, as one so often sees in that fair land of song, and wine, and old renown. The owner, who handed in his checks twenty years ago, had commenced building it when the city was a baby, a mere infant in arms; a bud, as it were, which was to blossom and bare rare fruit—"*Pro-*

bate" fruit—at no distant day. San Francisco, like Rome, is built on seven hills—more or less, or mountains, rather. There is Mount Russian, Mount Telegraph, and Mount California—better known as "Nob Hill"—and Mount Clay, and Lone Mountain. The latter is occupied mostly by the dead. In the distance, like guardian spirits, towers Mount Tamalpias and Mount Diablo. The name of the latter does not affect the spirit. But, as I was saying, the owner of the house on the Terrace commenced by laying the foundation sill upon a rock. At that time it was a very unpretentious structure, consisting of but two modest rooms (the cave), cunningly fashioned, with two closets—and two windows, with two doors leading out upon the piazza—and a connecting door between the two rooms. This was quite room enough for two people, in those days of canvas-covered dwellings, for, if they got into any little misunderstanding—there were the two apartments —one for each to cool off in. But, as the owner grew, and waxed strong financially, and his family increased numerically, he added story after story to his castle, which extended back into, and up the side of the mountain, like an opulent trapper's lodge— pillared and porticoed all the way up, with many a winding stairway, outside and in.

But I shall confine myself to the two primitive rooms (the cave) and their occupants. We (there were two of us who lived in the cave) christened it the "Turtle Dovery," because the owner was just married when he took possession of the airy castle. Here he spent his "honey" moon, and possibly entered upon the "comb"—no "tellin'." I dwelt in one room of the Dovery, and Delilah Hawthorn dwelt in the other.

"Who's Delilah Hawthorn?" you ask. I knew it! You know me, and that ought to satisfy you, but no, you must needs know Delilah Hawthorn. Well, I mean to be patient under all *great* trials—you shall be gratified. Although her name was, and is, Delilah, yet she is not a Philistine. Her ancestors came over in the Mayflower, and no Philistine trod the decks of that devoted ship. Her father was a Presbyterian clergyman, and his father was a Presbyterian clergyman, and his father's father was a Presbyterian clergyman, and so on, a long line of straight-laced blue-bellies, running clear back to Adam.

"But why don't you call her *Miss* Hawthorn?" "That's just what I'm coming to. Won't you be quiet? How can I ever finish the description of my friend—which I have not begun—if you keep breaking in and interrupting me all the time? She liked to have me call her Delilah, and I liked to please her. Are you satisfied?"

Delilah, like myself, is a woman of uncertain age, a spinster, or she was at that time, a school-mistress by profession, from choice. She was not compelled to follow in the footsteps of any illustrious predecessors. She gravitated toward it naturally. But wages are small, and brains cheap, where she came from down East—and having heard of the fabulous prices paid "schoolmarms" in San Francisco, and *not* having heard of the fabulous uncertainty of a stranger, however well qualified, ever getting an appointment from the "School Board," she gathered up her drygoods and gleanings saved from her slender income during many years of the most rigid economy—and set her face toward the setting sun, where all her bright hopes soon set in uncertainty. Hundreds of names on the applicants' roll of the School Department appeared before hers (this is no exaggeration). Fearing that it might prove detrimental to her general health to abstain from food during the period of probation, between no school and school—for, like a Probate widow's expectations, it might be several years ere a vacancy would occur, wherein she could secure an appointment—she in the interim decided to resort to woman's weapon against a sea of troubles, the needle.

Ah! what brave battles have been waged with that deadly weapon against Want and Starvation. The swift destruction of sword, cannon, and bomb, are merciful beside it. They do not slay by inches. They do not wring out the life-blood in single drops.

I, like Samson, took to Delilah the moment I heard her history. Not because she was beautiful *now;* she might have been once, but it required a very elastic imagination to fill up the interstices in the valleys surrounding those lustreless gray eyes, and the hollows in those pinched cheeks, with sparkle and bloom. The long, lank figure looked as though it had never been even in embryo, or during gestation, or lactation—properly nourished. She had lived all her life among the hills of New England, where the stones are said to be so close together that the noses of the sheep have to be filed to prevent their starving. She had budded, blossomed, and faded an ungathered rose on the parent stem. During the cold of winter, and the heat of summer, she had dried in muscle, and stiffened in joints, as she industriously wrought in ideas and wool. Five days and a half each week, in sunshine and storm, had found her at her post, in the little

DELILAH HAWTHORN.

unpainted schoolhouse on the hill, tussling with "the three R's, and the evenings had found her, when not at church, crochetting upon the hearth, to the song of the cricket and a dream of a lover, perhaps, who never came.

Her case and mine appeared identical, at this particular moment. She was running after the School Department, I was running after the Probate Department—the beautiful Probate Department. Both full of promise! A profitable expenditure of time and good feelings in either case. But at this point all resemblance ceased in this particular direction between us. She was good and I was bad; she was patient, and I impatient; she was a Christian, and I—well, not very pious. How can piety and Probate go hand in hand? Absurd! Impossible! It can't be done! If she had been me, she would have been just like me—all the same. If I had been her I should have been just like her—all the same. Whenever people say to me, "If I were you I would do differently," they don't know what they are talking about, for they wouldn't. They would do just exactly as I do, if they were me, for the ass does not change his skin nor the pied goose her spots.

During a religious revival among the Close Communion Baptists in Upper Hardscrabble, the native place of Delilah, she was converted, and in spite of her desire to worship with her kindred she had united with that sect of believers. She was a staunch advocate of election and preordination; but whenever she touched upon these brimstone subjects I invariably cried out, "Oh spare me, I pray! Don't put me on the gridiron and toasting-fork of speculative punishment, for I am cooked clear through now, muscle, bones, and marrow, by the fires of Probate. The warmth of the lower region, with all its reputed sulphur, would be as a candle beside Probate heat. I know that you are one of the elect, and I am not; I know that you will be saved, and that I shall be damned. I am damned already by the Probate Court, and the immaculate judgment of that court, which to my mind takes precedence of the final judgment."

"Now Elizabeth!" she exclaimed.

"Don't call me Elizabeth! you know that's not my name. I've been robbed—no, I beg pardon! unburdened of care, I should say—for are not great riches a care, and a burden, and a snare?—of all I possess excepting the names I own; and now am I to lose one of them? or what is just as bad, have an addition, a kind of front stoop, built up in front of it that does not belong there? What right have I to add to or subtract from any one of my '*lawful*' names, however abject and unworthy they may be of me, without the help and countenance of Congress, or a minister of the gospel, or a justice of the peace? None at all!"

"You ought to be ashamed of yourself," she made answer, looking very warm, for Delilah has spirit if not temper, "for letting them christen you *Lizzie*. It is a mongrel perversion of the noble name of Elizabeth, and I desire to call you by that name."

"But that's not my name," I reiterated, and the air felt very close. "I might just as appropriately call your little dog 'Nellie'" (I beg pardon for not introducing her before), "Helen."

"How can you put yourself in the scales against a dog, Elizabeth?" Delilah exclaimed in great disgust.

"Well, then," I continued, "if you don't like the name of Lizzie, call me by my other *Christian* name, Marietta."

"No; Marietta is a foreign name and only fit for very young people at that. *You* are not a *merry* Etta at your time of life, a woman that has been twice married and twice in Probate. Etta is a little girl's name, a pet abbreviation."

"I know that," I made reply, while a disagreeable sensation in my throat almost strangled the remainder of the sentence; "but my father calls me *little* Etta to this day, and would if I were double the age I am now and had been husbanded four times, and probated as many."

"Elizabeth was my mother's name," continued Delilah, as though she had not been interrupted, and I honor, I revere it on her account. If you decline to gratify me, I shall call you Mrs. Stow."

Now, ladies of an uncertain age always delight in calling each other by their Christian (not Pagan) names, and in speaking of themselves as "*girls.*" And the higher they go in the ascending scale, the more tenacious they become. Therefore, to preserve unimpaired this pleasing fiction, I yielded, and to forever banish all formality between us, I replied: "Well, call me what you like, always providing it is not late to dinner." Thus that most important matter was laid forever between us.

Although Delilah was a spinster and I was and *am* a widow, we seemed to occupy the same position in the economy of life. We both belonged to the order of superfluous women and to the tribe strongminded; we were both in need at that moment, and both had great expectations; she was not fishing for a husband, I was not fishing for a husband; she was obliged to economize very closely, I was obliged to economize very closely; she owned a black and tan dog, I owned a black and tan dog. But here the simile ends, for her dog was a little mouse-and-tan lady dog, which had been christened in infancy, "Nellie," after its mother. She, Nellie, was as prim, old-fashioned, and old-maidish as her mistress. Delilah had smuggled her all the way from New England to San Francisco, under her waterproof. How she could ever after that look Charley Crocker or Leland Stanford in the face again, beats me. She said that the sharp-eyed porters on the "sleepers" knew well enough that she had some live animal hidden under her waterproof and eyeproof circular, by the way they looked at it, but they asked no questions. They undoubtedly took her to be a female naturalist who had got a rare, live, but deadly *saurian* under cover, and that was the reason they did not meddle with her or it.

After Delilah arrived in San Francisco and came to live in the "Dovery" she was in no way harassed and tormented about the *ownership* of her dog as I was about mine. My dog is of the heroic gender, and his name is Jack. Nellie did not approve of making acquaintances among her own species, and when Jack showed her any attentions she showed her teeth at him in much the same spirit that would have developed a like appearance in her mistress, at the amatory overtures of some man. When I playfully broached the subject of matrimony in the most delicate manner, to her one day, she quite alarmed me by the serious way in which she took it.

"*Me marry!*" she exclaimed, growing pale about the lips, "*me*, marry a great nasty man! n–e–v–e–r! I wed my profession years ago and I never shall be divorced from my first and *only* love to gratify any man. That's wedlock enough for me." When she said this with lips firmly pressed, hands clenched, teeth set, and brows knit, a horrible thought, purpose and determination seized me, and how it was persistently worked up and carried out these pages will hereinafter duly chronicle.

The next morning after I moved into the cave (it was a veritable cave with *tout le mond* atop of it), when I opened my door to get the gill of milk—left by my landlady's obliging milkman, with so much noise and circumstance, in the sleepiest part of the whole night—a pretty half-grown kitten with a white face, gray body, and mild yellow eyes, was waiting outside to get in, or else guarding the pint pail with its half pint of milk, I never have been able to decide which. But when she looked up and saw me she said "mew," for good-morning, like a well-mannered kitten. I at once invited her in and gave her a part of my gill of milk and some cold roast lamb for her breakfast.

I have always heard that it was a good omen to have a strange cat come to one's residence, and was pleased with this favorable augury thus early in my new home.

When it had finished its breakfast and had made its toilet, I asked it what its name was; but it remained silent: therefore I came to the conclusion that it had not been christened, and immediately repaired the oversight by naming it Polly. It took very naturally to its name and to me also; for, although, as I shortly learned, it was the property of my landlady, it spent all its time with me when I was at home, either basking in the sun on the piazza of the "Dovery," or sleeping on the table at my elbow.

In a few days another cat came. "A pair of good omens!" I exclaimed. The last one was a serious, motherly looking cat, and appeared to be always hungry. She complained incessantly, and flew at Nell, to the horror of Delilah who said:

"That's a dreadful cat, Elizabeth. I never in all my life have been partial to cats. They are treacherous creatures, and I hate treachery in any form. She is sure to claw Nellie, sometime, and put out an eye, unless you drive her off. *I* shan't feed her."

"But," I urged, "the cat is hungry. She has evidently got kittens, somewhere; but what rouses my compassion most of anything is that she looks like a Probate-widow cat. As soon as I can win her confidence by kindness, I shall inquire into her case. She shall not lack a friend."

"You'll get your eyes scratched out, too, if you are not careful," said Delilah. "How she fought you when you tried to take a part of the meat away from her which she had snatched from Nell, and when you stroked her back, didn't she growl, spit, lash her tail, and scratch your hand to the bone?"

"I admit all you say," I replied, "Sally" (I had given her a name, too) "is not very tractable, but she is not used to kind treatment, and does not understand what it means."

I was glad to have something to pet, for I had been obliged to send Jack over the bay to prevent him from being taken possession of by playful people, that thought that they could take better care of him than I could. Therefore I was free to exercise my fascinations upon Sally.

She never ventured inside my room, and if I commenced to pick her up, I very soon commenced to put her down. However, one evening, at the end of a fortnight perhaps from her first appearance, she came in of her own accord, and jumped up in my lap to my great surprise. I saw by her sad and anxious countenance that she was in trouble. My sympathies were at once aroused, and I said:

"Sally, my dear friend, what is it that troubles you?" There was a dark spot on the side of her nose which gave her a look as though she had just taken a liberal pinch of "Havana flavored" Gilroy snuff, and had forgotten to use her handkerchief after it. At this moment that particular dark spot worked nervously as she looked long and inquiringly into my eyes—as though she would fathom the innermost recesses of my heart; her long whiskers almost scintillated with electricity, she was wrought up to such a state of excitement. At length, summoning up all her courage, she said:

"I should like to repose confidence in some one, for I have great need of sound counsel at this moment."

"Do not hesitate for an instant," I exclaimed, encouragingly, as I stroked her back, scratched her ear, and cuddled her under the chin. "I am perfectly trustworthy, and shall take the liveliest interest in all your joys and sorrows." This assurance on my part appeared to satisfy her, for clearing her throat by a slight cough, as she turned away her head and held a paw over her mouth, she gave me the following history of herself, which I retail to you verbatim.

During the recital she shed tears copiously, using her tail for a handkerchief, and she was frequently interrupted by sobs.

"I am a widow," she said, "with five little ones on my paws to support. The estate of my beloved Thomas consists of a gopher hole, two rat-holes, a hay-loft and a mole-ranch,—which you will readily understand is an ample competency for the elegant maintenance of his bereaved '*relict*' and orphans. But there is a court called Probate—perhaps you '*people*' do not have that sort of court?" I assured her we did, and considered it a beautiful institution, on account of its absorption qualities. "Just so!" she continued. "Well, I have been in this court for months, and it takes nearly all my time and my darling little ones are left alone, cold and hungry, while I watch the cog-wheels of *justice* instead of watching rats and mice and my poor neglected children.

"Where is this court convened?" I questioned.

"A long, long way from here," she replied, slowly shaking her head and moving her tail in a very rapid manner.

"I too, am a Probate widow," I said, "and have spent the best part of the day in court for the last two years. therefore I am deeply interested in your case. I should like to accompany you to-morrow, if '*folks*' are admitted to your cat-courts.

"Certainly!" she replied, "if you can walk so far. It is a long way from here. You see cats are neither builders nor excavators, therefore they have to seek comfortable natural residences in hollow logs, trees, and caves, or depend upon man for artificial ones. It is important that a court room should be quiet, and Judge Yowler is very particular, therefore he holds his court in a deserted observatory on top of Mount Telegraph."

I arranged all the preliminaries with her that evening; told her to bring her young and growing family to me, etc., etc. After she had said "good-night" I prepared a nice place for the kittens in an apple-box, with a warm bed made out of the shreds and clippings of cotton cloth kindly furnished by Delilah, although she did not at all approve of the course I was taking. "For," said she, "we shall be overrun and eaten out of cave and home by cats." I, however, was deaf to all expostulations, as usual, and went my way rejoicing.

The next day found Sally and I with faces set in

the direction of Mount Telegraph. When we arrived at the observatory the court was already opened. Probate Judge Yowler, a sleek, well-fed Tom-cat, in a bag-wig and spectacles, presided with a great show of pomp and circumstance. Seated on both sides of a table, improvised out of a board, in front of him sat a long line of cat-counsel, all Toms. Ranged along the walls were the cat-widows and several half-grown cat-orphans, all in tears.

Soon after we had taken our seats, Widow Mouser's case was called. I was quite surprised to hear Sally answer to that name, for I had neglected to inquire what her real title was. It seemed that there were a great number of attorneys in the case, for nearly all that were present appeared to have a paw in it. After much caterwauling, and spitting, and faing, and arching of backs, and lashing of tails, and unsheathing of claws, it seemed to settle and cool down of itself, and of its own accord, without having arrived at any particular result, excepting this: The judge ordered that the gopher-hole be advertised for three consecutive weeks, in the *Evening Bulletin*, after which it must be sold at public auction to the highest bidder, to pay costs of court. At this announcement Sally wept aloud, and the judge sternly ordered her to be quiet or else vacate the premises, if she didn't want to be sent "*up*" for contempt of court.

I patted her on the back and told her to be of good cheer, for were not the two rat-holes, the hay-loft, and the mole-ranch left to her still? Mentioned the "darkest hour," the "longest road," and many other like consoling old adages, yet I knew I was holding out false hopes, that, in the jocose order of beautiful Probate, they too were destined, at no distant day, to travel the same highway to the auction-block, and for the same purpose—"*costs*."

Widow Birdketcher's case was next in order. The estate consisted of the plaza, the south side of Washington Street and the north end of Kearney and Dupont Streets, which took in a portion of the City Hall and a fragrant slice of the Chinese quarter. All the solicitors appeared in this case as well. After the usual tussle and uproar had subsided, the judge ordered that the half of the plaza go to the block by the same process and in company with the gopher-hole, at which a shower of sparks fell from the eyes of Widow Birdketcher, and a vivid flash of lightning coursed along her back and shooting off the end of her tail struck in the ground, fortunately, but so near the end councilman that he sprang into the middle of the table with a prolonged ker-wow, and the place was filled with the odor of singed fur.

"Order! Attention!" shouted Judge Yowler, turning half round on the "bench," and lashing the desk in front of him with his tail. Order being restored, he continued: "This is the last case for to-day, and a most important case it is. It *shall* be finished before we leave this court-room, gentlemen. It has been in court seventeen thousand years, and a day, and the day ends it. *This is the day!*"

I did not understand the cause of the great warmth of his manner; he seemed unusually agitated for one in his high position. He acted more like the leader of a cat orchestra on a neighboring roof, when the beauty of a perfect chord is impinged upon by an uncultivated voice, with no ear for heavenly harmonies, than he did like an immaculate Probate judge. It was evident that he had touched an inharmonious Probate chord, for all the solicitors had risen to their feet and there was a double rainbow of *backs*—one on each side of the table; and two banners of tails unfurled, and two double rows of teeth revealed. A prolonged growl arose, like the groan before a tempest, and each Tom-counsellor went in on his own hook. It appeared that disputes were settled in this court as they were in Germany four hundred years ago, by strength of muscle instead of strength of argument. The contest was a lively one. The air in the vicinity of the table was filled with fur, briefs, inkstands and penholders, and there was electricity enough in the room to set North River and Puget Sound on fire. Every eye and back was aflame with it. The judge had abandoned his dignity and taken an active part in the fray from the first. His bag-wig had been clawed off at the outset, and tossed over among the widows, where it was received in much the same spirit that a mad dog would have been. They spit at it, tossed it from one to another, sat down in it, kicked at it, and in every way showed the contempt they felt for its "*upright*" owner—the white Ermine.

Not knowing where the fracas would end, and fearing that it might become general and involve the widows, I begged Sally to excuse me as I had a "pressing engagement." Thus I made my escape. When she came home at night she presented a sorry sight. There was a ghastly wound on her head, caused, she informed me, by her having forgotten that she was sitting in the judge's bag-wig, until she was forcibly reminded of it by the strong right paw of that all-powerful cat functionary.

I then persuaded her to go to court no more, for

it availed nothing and it was only a loss of time; that in the end she would get her deserts—millions of gopher-holes and billions of mole-ranches, well-stocked; that all "Toms" were the natural *protectors* of cat-widows and cat-orphans in general, and Tom-solicitors and Tom-judges in particular; that her sphere was home attending to her little ones, etc. And I am happy to inform my readers that she heeded my advice, and ever after emulated the Roman matrons in home duties.

With Sally's consent I named all her little ones. Being greatly exercised over the presidential election—because I had no part to play in it, probably—and taking the liveliest interest in both candidates, I christened the two handsomest kittens Rutherford B. Hayes and Samuel J. Tilden, respectively. Rutherford B. was the finest of the lot, and he soon became a great favorite of mine. When I went away in the morning to sell "Probate Confiscation," he would accompany me half-way down the long flight of stairs leading from the "Turtle Dovery" to the street —Rosin Street—and when I returned at night after having sold "Probate Confiscations," or rather several copies of it, he would come half-way down the stairs to meet me, saying: "Mew, mew, mew," which to my sophisticated ears meant, "How dy' do! Glad to see you! Come right in! I'm dying for a frolic! Mother has taken Sam hunting, and Bigeye and all the rest are asleep—the stupid things! and Nell's cross, and I am literally dying of *ennui*."

I had attached—a well-placed attachment—my round ball of a pen-wiper to a strong string, and after the cares of the day were ended used to frolic by the

SALLY AS AN EDUCATOR.

hour with the playful kits. Great minds are always pleased and entertained with simple amusements. It afforded me almost as much pleasure as it would have done if I had had a *fool* to talk to. An acquaintance of mine said that his earthly happiness would be complete if he had a fool, instead of an intelligent wife, to talk to after the labors of the day were done.

Rutherford B. was gray with a white setting, while Samuel J. was a tortoise-shell cat in miniature. The white kitten with a black ear, I named Bobbins, on account of its marvellous agility at ball-playing, and the two others, Boz and Bigeye. The latter got his cognomen from the peculiar way he opened his eyes, and from his being a consummate glutton. He always managed to get his right eye wider open than his left, and he also managed to get double his share of meat and milk. As soon as this interesting family were well acquainted with Nellie, they became fast friends; and then the days and nights on the terrace were enlivened by the playful pranks of the six kittens. Sally had profited by my advice and had not been to court since she was wounded by Judge Yowler, and she had become as playful and light of heart as the youngest one of the lot.

Delilah was nearly as much interested in them as I was. We took a quart of milk between us, now, to meet the growing necessities of our large family. Sometimes it was stolen, for thieves and burglars were becoming alarmingly plentiful about that time. We took great precaution, so as not to be surprised by them, at night, by fastening down our windows and barricading our doors with gimlets, and corkscrews, and stilettoes, and scissors, and penknives, and hair-pins, and nails, and forks. We had one apiece of the latter, and when sister Gertie came over from Oakland to attend a matinee, and we had a *déjeuner à la fourchette* before going, I had to eat with the brad-awl.

One bright moonlight night, the very time for burglars and desperadoes to operate on a terrace, I heard one scratching and digging away at the blind. He had evidently forced himself in at the bottom of the raised sash, and was working his way up between the inside shutters and window pane, by the way the blinds rattled. I sat up in bed, which was opposite and facing the window, and taking my revolver, which I always keep under my pillow at night, and which contains the same charge that was taken to Europe in it in '74, I prepared for the worst by cocking the deadly, although I fear somewhat rusty weapon, but coolly reserving my fire until the ruffian and midnight assassin's head should show itself above the blind. I was none too quick about it, for the head came over the lower blind just as I got my fingers upon the trigger, and two glowing eyes looked straight at me, and then a body followed the head and glowing eyes, and then head, glowing eyes and body sprang down on to the table under the window, and with another desperate leap the trio landed upon the bed. I did not fire, I did not scream, I did not faint, I simply said, "Why, Polly, ain't you ashamed of yourself, to give me such a fright?" But the moment the cat, it was a cat, purred and rubbed, and rasped himself upon the bed-spread, and chucked his head under my chin, I knew that it was not Polly— Polly was not a demonstrative cat—but a strange cat, another "*omen*," and such an omi-

THE DEADLY WEAPON.

nous tail as it had! The hair was so thick upon it that it stood out in a whorl like a lamp-chimney brush; and when the owner of the tail purred, it was grand. Such a purr as that cat had! it was like the sound of many waters.

When Delilah saw him she said, "I told you so! One cat tolls another. The terrace is covered with them every night, and such a noise as they make! It is enough to wake the dead."

"Well," I replied—I always say "*well*," when I have no other argument at hand—"it is a good omen and one more can't make much difference either way. I shall christen him Bismarck, he is such a persistent, resolute, fearless fellow. He makes only *seven* in all that belongs to *us*. Polly, you know, is not our cat. Seven is my lucky number, therefore I hail the advent of Bismarck as an ominous cat-climax. There will come no more cats to the "Turtle Dovery" for adoption, see if there does!" And my prophecy was correct.

"Then if no more comes this will prove the seven wonders; but to my mind it will prove a cat-astrophy," continued Delilah, with an ominous shake of the head.

"Most likely," I replied laughing. "This seventh son

A PAIR OF REVOLVERS.

of a seventh son is evidently a Russian cat, brought down the coast by some vessel which plies between this port and Alaska. No San Francisco cat ever grew such a warm covering as he has got on his back. Just feel of it, and see if it is not genuine polar-fur."

Bismarck proved to be a very sociable cat, and when he was spoken to always answered with an intelligent sparkle in his big round eyes. He made right up to Nell, purring and rubbing his sides against her, and they became good friends immediately; slept in the same basket, and ate of the same plate; and Delilah forgot all about cat-treachery. He went up-stairs on a tour of inspection the next morning, after he arrived so unceremoniously in the dead of night, and when he came down he was decorated with a gay order in the form of a blue ribbon tied in a bow-knot under his aldermanic chin; but after a few days he returned from one of those friendly calls as wet as Euphemia was when she was taken from the brook by her adorable Augustus, where she had fallen in her ambition to catch "*trouts*" collectively. When an inquiry of "Why?" was set on foot, it was proved, beyond a doubt, that Bismarck had gone up on the piazza several times during the night and serenaded the ungrateful sleepers, who symbolized their appreciation of the varied melody by a bucket of water dashed over the performer.

Mr. Wimple called soon after the seventh addition to our impromptu family had got well established in his new quarters. Mr. Wimple was a mutual friend

LIVING IN THE CAVE.

BISMARCK IN A BROWN STUDY.

and our only constant gentleman caller. He often dropped in of an evening to have a quiet cut-throat rubber. Mr. Wimple was a little old, dried-up, musty, fusty bachelor—a bookworm by profession. He had lived among books all his life. *Old* books were his delight. He was a kind of unabridged antiquarian book naturalist, and carried the odor of his profession about with him, like a taxidermist or a freshman in anatomy. Delilah declared that she could smell him a block and a half away. But then Delilah had a nose for smells; a sharp, thin, penetrating nose that never missed a smell where there was one to be had. He never remembered anything which was not written in a book. You might tell him of the dangerous condition of your mother-in-law, or of a financial windfall or any other dire calamity a dozen different times, and he would still exclaim, "Is it possible? You surprise me! Can such things be!" And if I happened to casually mention the sublime labors of the upright executors of my late husband's last will and testament, and the noble bearing and urbane deportment of the judge of Probate, his ecstasy knew no limit, his admiration no bounds. He would jump up out of the armchair—I had an arm-chair in my room in the cave—clap his hands together in an ecstasy of delight, thrust them under his coat-tails, and pace up and down the room—not a long range—saying "Splendid fellows! they understand how to squeeze an estate till the ducats roll in a shower at their feet. Prime fellows! Lucky dogs! And Myrick, he's a trump card, a diamond trump; he's never on the wrong side. Always wins! Wonderful financiers—all!" After he had quite exhausted himself by walking and talking, and turning and smiling—Mr. Wimple, I say it in confidence, Mr. Wimple was short of breath—would sit down again in the arm-chair and twirl his eye-glasses and thumbs. Twirling thumbs and eye-glasses was a habit of Mr. Wimple's. He could not sit still unless his thumbs were in motion.

But, as I was saying, our friend Wimple called. It was a glorious night. The moonlight flooded the terrace and lit up the "Dovery" in mystic splendor. The heart of the city, beyond and beneath our commanding site, with its million gas-jets, looked like a sparkling gem. A wreath of snow frosted the eastern horizon, lying upon the Coast range like foam upon the billow. On the west towered "Nob Hill," with its red-wood palaces. What more was wanting to perfect the picture? Nothing.

Mr. Wimple, as he unwound a shawl from about

his neck, said, "You have it all your own way up here, ladies. You are almost as isolated as you would be in the centre of the Atlantic."

"True," I made answer, "we might be murdered and no one would be the wiser, we are so far above the street and the house proper is so far above us that a cry for help would be futile."

"But what a colony of cats you've got," he continued; "enough to stock the city."

"That's so," chimed in Delilah, "but Elizabeth calls them her 'good omens' and won't part with one of them, as long as she stays in the 'Dovery.' They are very happy here and really very much attached to her. The way they fly down the steps when they hear her voice is something wonderful. They are certainly very knowing cats and appreciate a true friend."

"Exactly!" ejaculated Mr. Wimple with an eloquent eye cast in the direction of the little card-table. It was soon brought out and the game commenced in earnest. Next to books, I think Mr. Wimple loved cards the best of anything in the world. He played a careful hand, with an eye to Wimple, and would brook no nonsense.

The cats were all out on the piazza drinking milk or moonshine, and occasionally getting very hilarious over it, judging from the sounds that floated through the open window. But no sooner had Bismarck caught the tones of a man's voice than he bounded through the window, and before poor, precise little Wimple understood the situation Bismarck was in his lap, rubbing and purring at the top of his very strong purr-voice.

Mr. Wimple was probably one of the best groomed men in San Francisco. A cat or a dog hair never found peaceful lodgment on any part of his wearing apparel. "Scat, scat!" he shouted, standing up and dislodging the foe, but the instant he—Wimple—sat down again, Bismarck renewed his friendly overtures. I was obliged to put him out and close the blinds, but he had not forgotten his first *entrée* and his head soon appeared at the top of the blind.

"What a remarkable cat!" exclaimed Mr. Wimple, as he trumped my ace of hearts, "I would suggest the closing of the window." This done, Bismarck took up his post at the door, and such an unearthly complaint as he set up, rackurrowing, purrthurmewing, and kerrowing, moved the heart of even Mr. Wimple to pity, and Bismarck was allowed to come in. But he was very uneasy. I at last set a chair for him at the table, changed the game to whist, and for sport dealt him a dummy.

To our great delight he was perfectly at home in the game—that accounted for his persistent determination to get in—knew every card and played a most skilful (paw) hand. The only drawback in his case, and I am happy to say we took no advantage of it, was, he spread his cards out on the table before him in full view of all of us, and selecting the desired one, he shoved it into place with his right paw. I was his partner and, of course, drew in the tricks. I played wrong several times, to see if he would know it. I have strong reasons for thinking that he did know it, by the way he stood up in the chair, with tail erect, and glaring eyes, as he held down his cards with one paw, and shook the other angrily at me. He had seen lively times over the card table, wherever he received his education, in all probability.

"That cat," said Mr. Wimple, "has been brought up in a camp, and could teach us many a trick if he thought it worth his while. All animals are much more intelligent than they appear to be."

"You are right there," I replied. "Du Chaillu's two black cats always accompanied him on all his scientific rambles, and their timely aid saved his life several times from venomous reptiles, and poisonous animals. If he neglected to light the gas in the stove in a little laboratory, where his dusky pets slept at night, a sharp blow on the side of his head, administered by a vigorous paw, brought him to a sense of feeling upon the pleasurable sensations of warmth to a well-bred cat.

When I was in Sacramento in '66, paying my respects to the Legislature, I made the acquaintance of a bachelor who had sown and harvested all his wild oats—not a large crop—and had grown tired of his "blessed" lot and of himself, *single*. He sighed long and loud for a housekeeper (he had a home), a button-fastener, a stocking mender, and a constant companion to listen to his home-spun yarns, about his deeds of daring in crossing the plains, in mining camps, and of hairsplitting escapes from wild "Injuns," wild animals, and all kinds of uncivilized dangers, which he—more than any other man alive—had encountered, and come off first best, single-handed and alone. He didn't want *me*. Oh no! he preferred some unsophisticated creature who had never experienced the joys of wedlock and the bliss of having a "protector."

"Not much!" he said very emphatically, in order to have firm ground between us, "none of your knowing old foxes for me—*if you please*. I don't expect to get a young girl to marry an old fogy like me, I hain't got rocks enough for that; but some clever, sensible woman, who wants a roof of her own over her head, might hitch horses, if she wasn't particular about beauty." Here he gave an awful snort —which I echoed, somewhat to the embarrassment and surprise, no doubt, of the speaker. "However," he continued, after he had felt of his chin, and given a tug or two at the long grizzly bristles that adorned it—I have often noticed, that some men in a quandary always resort to their chins to help them out of it; others to their legs, which they caress—or trot, trot, trot; then, again, others turn to their thumbs, which they twirl, and twirl, and twirl, looking as foolish and pleased as possible. I have tried all these means when I didn't feel good, and found them exasperating failures. I have coddled my chin, trotted my foot, and twirled my thumbs by the half hour, but the experiments brought no relief. I have even gone so far as to try the effect of looking in the mirror, to see if it

EBENEZER HERRING.

did not mollify my countenance somewhat; but no, it seemed to grow glummer, the faster I twirled, trotted, or coddled.

"However," he continued, "I've got along purty comfortably so far, and expect I can manage the rest of the way tolable well."

"Mr. Herring," I exclaimed—Herring is his mister name. He has another, but it is not necessary to tell what it is just yet. "Mr. Herring, you have no right to deprive some good woman of a good home, and a good husband. There are hundreds of poor homeless creatures in California, who would jump at the chance of becoming mistress of your house, Herring and all. I'll help you out on this line, if it takes all summer. I'm good at match-making, that is, I have assisted quite successfully at two."

"Do you really mean what you say?" he broke in, looking at me in a half amused, half earnest, quizzical sort of way, out of those weasel-eyes of his, which, for the moment, nearly convulsed me with laughter. Recovering my equilibrium, somewhat, I replied, "Certainly! if you are in earnest."

"I'm blamed if I ain't," he said, musingly, and half to himself, "and you shall be first bridesmaid and dance at the wedding. Here's my hand as a pledge!"

"I'll take the hand, providing there's no heart in it," I laughingly replied, and so the matter ended, for the time being.

After my return from the capital city, I had been kept in such rapturous ecstasy over the joys of beautiful Probate, and my unspeakable admiration of upright executors, that all remembrance of the playful promise had faded out of my memory, until Delilah's most positive and energetic decision brought it before my mind's eye in all its freshness of coloring and beauty of detail.

"Splendid!" I mentally ejaculated. "Here is a rare combination—real fun and real philanthropy united. They do not often go together, but in this case they are inseparable correlatives. These people were made for each other. They look enough alike to be brother and sister. Husbands and wives always look alike. In that respect, they resemble the old lady's son Bijah. She had several sons, but none of them looked alike but Bijah, and he looked *just alike:* so the old lady said.

"I must net these rare old specimens of ornithology," I said to myself, very determinedly, "in one net; trap them in one trap; snare them in one snare. I will write Herring all the particulars, and invite him down to the Bay. He has a merry vein in him, and will enjoy the lark, if it don't come to any lasting result. He needs a holiday; he has got money, and is not afraid to spend it. In the interim, I will so expatiate upon the joys of wedlock, and the paradise of home, and the dearth of a lonely life, that this forgotten bud of promise shall blossom and bear fruit before the new year assumes his crown and sceptre."

I wrote my letter, and in due time my "*beau*," as I sportively called him in my "talks" with Delilah, arrived. He looked very shiny in a new suit of broadcloth, fresh soft crown and light kids. We had a merry time for a week. We drove in the parks, to the Cliff, and did Oakland, and lunched at my sister's on San Pablo avenue. She was thoroughly posted and entered into the "catch" with great glee. The cold collations provided by her for the occasion would have melted and warmed the hearts of two stones, that is, if they had been hungry stone hearts.

My sister, unlike her sister, is an admirable cook, and she does not wholly eschew her own kitchen. A nosegay of pansies, sweet peas and heartsease was laid beside either plate, while from a centre vase in the middle of the table trailed, bloomed and perfumed the choicest, loveliest, sweetest posies imaginable. Ah! what a gorgeous and enjoyable lunch it was, with my handsome, dark-eyed sister, my mother's youngest born, the "*little one*" of my father's household, sitting at the head of the table and doing the honors like a fairy queen, while we, her willing subjects, felt and acted too just like the "*merrie*" people of the greenwood. Bottom's and Titania's pranks were quite cast into the shade by our merry-making. Every one was laughing, even to Jack. He sat beside me on the floor—of course. Did you think a cover was laid for him? He laughed till his lips were drawn clear back to his ears. The "healths" and the "long life" that were drank that day, if but a fraction were realized, would cause a rivalry with the reputed years of Methuselah. The pleasure-seekers and the feast got very much mixed along toward the last of it. Gertie, that is my sister's Christian name, declared that she found some of Delilah's jelly on the ceiling after we were gone. "What of that?" I said; "I insisted upon her drinking my health, and the health of the Probate court of San Francisco, and the health of the Probate judge, the white Ermine of San Francisco, after she said her head was light as a feather, and that she never drank a drop of champagne before in her life. But Mr. Herring assured her that champagne never got into the head but into the heels, and that if she did not feel like dancing then she was not under its influence. I know that when she cut up her silver cake that half of it flew across the table into my lap. But then, what of that? I like silver cake and was glad to get it. I had an attraction for it and it had an attraction for me, else it would not have come my way. It enabled me to take my piece home in my pocket for my next day's lunch."

We went to the opera and theatre, always taking Delilah with us, although she protested, and said that lovers—*Lovers !* Herring and I lovers !—should always be by themselves and not have the admixture of the disagreeable third party.

Soon after our gallant escort had gone home, Delilah broke silence—one evening as we sat looking at each other, and resting, she from her sewing machine, I from my Confiscation bouts — by saying, "What a very nice, agreeable man Mr. Herring is ! I almost wonder that he has remained single all his life. What a pity that his name is Herring." ("It is beginning to work," said I to myself, hardly able to keep my face straight.) "I would appeal to Congress and have it changed if I were he, before afflicting any woman with it."

"Nonsense!" replied I, "you would have it changed to Whale, I suppose. What's in a name? A Herring by any other name would smell as sweet."

"What's his other name?" she continued; "that may make amends for this."

"I'm not so certain about that, although it is a Christian and a Bible name—Ebenezer."

"Ebenezer Herring! worse and worse. Herring was bad enough, but to have such a prefix as Ebenezer is simply monstrous. I could never abide the name of Ebenezer."

"I see nothing very dreadful about the name; a wife usually calls her hubby, for a time at least, a pet name, and Mr. Herring's wife could call him Ebby, or Neezy, or she might call him Johnny or Charley without materially affecting Congress."

"Stuff! One likes to be called by his true name," she impatiently replied.

"I would not be exacting if I were you," said I, "after your persistency in building an upright to my name. It is the person and the home that I look at, and not the name. He is not handsome, but he has got a handsome home that lacks nothing but a good mistress to convert it into another Eden. It is the duty of every one to lend their aid to the building up of permanent homes. They are the foundation-sill of the nation—the fulcrum of all that is most worthy and beautiful in society. If I should never marry again, I shall, some time, make a home for myself and a shelter for others, and thus become a more substantial factor in the economy of life."

"Yes," she responded, almost bitterly, "you can do it, because you have the means; but I can't. I shall live in pigeon-holes, for I cannot afford to live differently, until I am old enough to be admitted to the 'Old Ladies' Home.'"

"Not a very cheering outlook, I confess! But why have you set your face so defiantly against wedlock?"

"Elizabeth!" she exclaimed quite fiercely, "I never had an offer of marriage in my life, nor a lover either. All the enterprising young men in the town and country where I was born, and have always lived until I came here, went 'West' as soon as they shed their milk teeth, and I am not the only one that cried 'heigho for a husband' when the bloom was on the rye."

"Delilah, you are a true, sensible woman, and I should like to see you well settled in life. You cannot expect to be carried away with the delirium of intoxicating passion—oftentimes mistaken for love—at your age and with your experience. What is love? It is something that develops a beautiful friendship which outlives youth and beauty, bloom and sparkle, gray hairs and wrinkles. Love sports in the garden of pleasure, or that which is called love, amid bloom and sensuous beauty, fanned and caressed by summer airs. It toys with the exquisite, but perishable casket, without a thought or care about the hidden jewel which it contains. But friendship penetrates to the gem within, the deathless spirit which should grow more and more valuable, more and more beautiful as the casket fades, and becomes old and ugly to all eyes but those of true friendship. I know of a beautiful home which has no mistress. Within that home is a faded casket, weather-stained and storm-beaten, but it contains the precious jewel of a noble soul, true as tried gold; and here is another faded and fortune-tossed casket, with its priceless jewel," I continued, laying my hand tenderly on her shoulder, " which jewel I should like to see shining where it would give more light, and do more good than it can living for itself alone, simply existing, hidden in a pigeon-hole."

As I ceased speaking, Delilah turned a little gold circlet upon her finger, but did not speak. The little worn thread of gold was her mother's wedding-ring.

"Come!" said I, starting up so suddenly that I upset Bismarck and Nellie. They had been attentive auditors. "Let's be off to dinner. It is so nice to go half a mile and eat at a restaurant among all sorts of people instead of in one's own home, among those we love and from one's own board, covered with spotless damask, polished silver, and shining cups; with a rare vase of Hawthorn blossoms on one side of it and a Herring on the other."

As we were returning from the restaurant we encountered a creature in the semblance of man on the sidewalk, laboring under the effects of too much tangle-foot. He evidently mistook his vile, bloated carcass for a rubber ball, by the way he tossed it about; here against a lamp-post or hitching-post, there against the fence or the wall of a building. His hat was dragged down over one eye, and the other was winking, while the repulsive mouth, that a mother had once kissed, was gibbering incessant nonsense. A loathsome, breathing pestilence, on the face of the fair earth.

"Oh, dear suz a me!" cried Delilah, as soon as he was within range of her vision. Delilah was short-sighted, or *near*-sighted, I believe that is what it is called, when a person cannot tell his sweetheart from his prospective mother-in-law, across the street.

Delilah never confessed the infirmity, and she never wore her massive gold-bowed spectacles in the street. At first I attributed this to be a precautionary measure, on her part, against being waylaid by street garroters and despoiled of her treasure. She set a great "store" on those old-fashioned spectacles, for they were a sort of visionary heirloom in the Hawthorn family. They were brought over from Old England in the Mayflower, and they have been descending in a straight line ever since.

"Don't you see that drunken man, Elizabeth? What a dreadful creature!" To make certain that I heard her, she grasped hold of my pull-back pocket, in which was a hot sweet potato, that I was taking home for my next day's dinner.

"Goodness gracious alive!" she exclaimed, catching her breath with a gasp and losing all anxiety about the tippler, who at that moment was hugging a telegraph pole in a maudlin, sentimental sort of way, and leering, and ducking, and talking at us. I heard between the indignant protests of my companion, "Charm (hic) in' (hic) old (hic) gals (hic)." "Goodness gracious alive, Elizabeth! has this probate business blunted all your sense of right and wrong?"

"Possibly!" I made reply. "If it had, that

would be one of the least of its playful eccentricities. But I do not understand you. Please explain."

"How did you get that sweet potato into your pull-back pocket without exposing the—what shall I call it?—*moral obliquity*—to the whole dining-room?"

"I made no bones of the sweet potato; I told the waiter that I wanted it to take home to help make a stew for my dinner, to-morrow."

"But you didn't pay for it!"

"No, not directly. But if I had eaten the '*moral obliquity*' there, you would have considered that I had paid for it."

"How can you be so irreverent, Elizabeth, as to call a sweet potato a *moral obliquity?*"

"That's what you called it!"

"No, no! you are mistaken, it was the *act*."

"I can see no difference," I continued, "if you are served with a sweet potato at a restaurant, whether you eat it there or take it home to eat when you have a better appetite."

"What a remarkable view you take of things, Elizabeth! You might just as appropriately take the spoons, platters, and pitchers, as to take the food."

"No, I pay two bits for three plates of food and *et-cæteras*, but I do not pay for the platters and plates upon which that food is served. Now, if I find from any cause, that it will be more for my interest to appropriate that portion which is not consumed at the sitting, what is the difference between eating it then and there, or now, or hereafter?"

"The difference is very marked, as I look at it. If the proprietor knew it, and approved it, that would change the complexion of the deed entirely" ("Make it lighter colored,") I mused parenthetically. "Little did I think when you were paying your two bits at the counter, and buying a short-bit loaf of bread, and talking about the weather as though butter wouldn't melt in your mouth—that you had a sweet potato in your pull-back pocket. Why didn't you show it to Mr. Myres?"

"But why should I have shown him this particular sweet potato? He had seen it before, probably, so there would have been no novelty about it. He sees sweet potatoes every day, and eats them too, most likely. I am fond of all sweet things. Sweet potatoes were made to be eaten. They grew and were nourished by our common mother Earth. We are all her children, both animals and vegetables."

"From such deductions I arrive at the conclusion, that the sweet potato in your pull-back pocket is a kinsman of mine?"

"Certainly! Are we not born of the same universal mother? Are we not nourished at the same universal breast during life, and at death does she not wrap her universal mantle around us (and give us over to the tender mercies of the universal worm) when we lie down with kings, the wise, the good—

'All in one mighty sepulchre'?"

Having arrived at the foot of the long flight of steps leading up to the "Dovery," the conversation was cut short from my abruptly changing the subject, by saying—"Go up first, Delilah; Beauty before Age." I always requested her to precede me up stairs, knowing that if she were to lose her balance, or footing—or faint, and should fall a-top of me, that there would be no great harm done, she being such light weight, but were such a mishap to befall me while leading the van, woe to the followers! for something or somebody would be out and injured.

When we stood on the piazza of the Cave to recover the breath which twenty-six steps upward had taken away, we were struck, as we never failed to be, with the beauty of the outlook. The moon, in its zenith of glory, was just lifting its face from the shimmering silver of the bay, the beautiful bay! With the speed of a freed spirit, my thoughts bore me back to Naples and Sorrento, when, on such a night as this, I crossed from Sorrento to Naples in a kind of yacht manned by six young Neapolitans, who sang by my request, the soft delicious melodies of that melodious clime, to the tune of oar-beat and heart-beat, until "the haunted chambers of the night" were a-blossom with sweet sounds. The oarsmen were as supple and beautiful in physical development and bare-foot grace—as Apollos. I saw again, by introversion, Vesuvius, grand and awful, crowned with lurid light and plumed with smoke. I saw the blue dome arching above, fretted with westward-going stars, while the moon, like a mailed maiden, was riding in the van.

"Slowly the bright procession went down the gleaming arch,
And my soul discerned the music of their long triumphant march,
Till the great celestial army, stretching far beyond the poles,
Became the eternal symbol of the mighty march of souls."

I saw again the dark outline of the olive-browed hills against the matchless splendor of Italia's heaven; I saw the city with her countless lights, a radiant gem set in fadeless emerald; and I saw myself sitting in the stern of the fairy boat, dipping my hand in the cool water, and watching the riffle-ribbon that followed it as it parted, for an instant, the yielding mirror that made two worlds of one.

"What a perfect night!" said my companion, breaking in upon my visionary reverie.

"Yes," I replied. "I wonder if Heaven will be any more enjoyable to our spiritual vision than some parts of earth are to our mortal ken?"

"I shall be satisfied if it is," she abstractedly replied.

"There is something about the bay of San Francisco," I continued, "which always reminds me of the bay of Naples. They are alike in their amplitude of expanse and their amphitheatre of hills. Diablo's old head yonder may sometime blossom in flame and smoke; and San Rafael and San Quintine may yet become as much of pilgrim shrines as Pompeii or Herculaneum. The modern Diomede of San Rafael would make a more substantial relic than the calcine-fused Roman or his associates do."

When Mr. Herring said "good-bye" on leaving San Francisco, he promised to write to us sometime when he "felt like it," that is, when he was in a communicative mood; and Mr. Herring fulfilled his promise, as the following *exact* copy of his letter will show.

SACRAMENTO, OCT. 15, '76.

DEAR FRIENDS:—How d'y do? How's the " Dovery ?" How are Nell and the seven cats? How's the weather? Had any more champaign lunches? Bouffed any since we saw Aimee— in what do you call it?—The Jolly Perfumer? Wasent it jolly, though? Arn't you sick of being alone? I am sea-sick, love-sick, home-sick, and self-sick, altogether. I'm lousemer 'n ever since that visit. Wish it hadn't been made. No, I'm blamed if I do! Dident we have a tip-top old time, us old cronies? Just the ones to know how to enjoy a good time. But I wont stand this! I *wont!*—so there, and there it shall end—*down there!!!* My foot's down and that means biz. I cant ask you both to turn into salt-water fish--smoked and dried at that—although my heart's big enough for both, and there are rooms enough in this lonesome old shanty for three to tiff in. No objection whatever to a modest supply of that sort of thing. A little lightning clears the atmosphere, and then I've hearn tell that the making up is as delightful as a tea-party or candy-pull.

Now old girls I'm coming down to the Bay again, next week— *mind!* So hang on the pot and get up the "fixins," and be lively about it, for by the great horn spoon's I'm going to marry one or both of you. I wish we were Utahans. But seeing we aint, here goes——

"Delilah Hawthorn will you marry me, Ebeneezer Herring, bachelor? Will you be my lawful wedded wife till death do us part? Will you barter your thorn for a Herring? If so, then Barkis is willin' and ready to jump over the first broomstick he comes to. He could rival the famous cow, in agility, should the temptation be a honey-moon. If it is all hunky dory, Lizzy shall give away the bride (woman's rights, you know), and toss up the slipper, and kiss the groom, *you bet!*'" You needn't write, I'll receive sentence *viva voce.*

Yours in the throes of love,
EBEN HERRING.

As I finished reading the letter and laid it on the table, I remarked, with perfect nonchalance: "Eben Herring is a handsome name written. There is nothing fishy about the looks of it. H is one of the prettiest letters in the alphabet, and that you will retain all the same. Now about the '*fixins.*' We must arrange all the preliminaries to-night, the time is so short. *Just like a man!* Men seem to think the world was made in a day instead of six. In the morning we will go down town to Mosgrove's and buy the dress. Such lovely shades as he has got: ashes of roses, mist on the bay, moonlight on the lake, fog on the hills, sunshine on the sea, haze on the mountains, and bloom on the rye. Just the things for a mature bride. I declare, when I saw them in the window I almost felt like getting married myself."

"*Elizabeth*," broke in Delilah, "what *are* you talking about? Have you gone stark mad?"

"No, my dear," I replied, "I am deferring that important period of my life (although some have maintained, after a careful perusal of Probate Confiscation, that it had arrived already) until I come into possession of the colossal fortune which is at the present moment being disintegrated by the white-heat zeal of self-sacrificing executors, aided and abetted by the Probate judge, and all the Probate fraternity, whose name is *legion*. They will soon have the free gold separated from the dross, for no refractory estate can stand the furnace of Probate more than seventy thousand years; and then, when this result is accomplished, I shall go quietly mad in the most approved and orthodox manner possible.

"But, as I was saying, about the dress and the new outside garment? I have it! Your bridal gift from me shall be that Paisley shawl of mine with the white centre, that you admire so much. I expect, every time I unfold it, to find a moth in it."

"I shall not accept it," she said slowly, "and rob you of an expensive garment that you will wear sometime, if you do not now."

"Bravo! she accepts the offer, though!" I responded, mentally. "Well, well, we'll see!" I continued audibly. "Now about the trimmings to the dress. There's that *point d'appliqué* and white gimp that was on my rose silk, they are just the thing. The dress was given away long ago, and the trimming is becoming jaundiced from neglect. Now it shall see daylight and the *amende honorable.* And gloves? How fortunate that we wear gloves the same size! I have a box that I bought in Paris, which has never been opened. You see I mean to relieve you of all care as regards detail and management. I shall have the 'Rev. Cream Cheese' perform the ceremony, and invite Mr. Wimple to stand up with me as first groomsman."

Suffice it to say, I was up with the lark the next morning, built the "fire," and hung on the "pot," and kept up a roaring blaze under it, until by the end of the week everything was cooked, dried, and ready for use. The *silk*, a lovely gray with the faintest blush of rose, embellished with creamy lace and gimp, lay in my top bureau drawer, which had been "rid up" for that very purpose. In the hat-box of my trunk, nestled in its garniture of lace and hawthorn blossoms a "love of a bonnet," made out of a piece of the pink-tinted gray. I found a pair of gloves, on opening my fresh box, that the silk must have been matched to when it was dyed. Side-laced gaiters were made from the silk, and a natty parasol was covered with it, and still there was a yard left over for a new waist. I always calculate for the yard over.

"Eben," said Delilah, she had taken quite kindly to "Eben," seeing that she disliked abbreviations so much, "Eben will find he's got a gray goose instead of a thorn."

Sister Gertie sent over a two-bushel basket of cut flowers and a bride's cake with cupids skipping up their heels on the frosting, and a pair of hearts pierced through and through the centre by an arrow, and under the hearts were clasped hands, and a true-lover's knot and turtle doves cooing, which made it very beautiful to look at. But the beauty of the outside could not rival the delicacy of the inside. My sister had made it with her own hands out of superfine flour—"best brand"—fresh butter, sweet cream, unadulterated sugar and fresh eggs. My sister's hens laid the eggs, and my sister's hens never lay any other than fresh eggs. I am not so positive about the cream. My sister does not keep a "pretty cow," as a bride elect (not our bride) anticipated that she should do when they—she and her ancient Benedict, that was to be—went to live in a "pretty cottage" in the country.

"Oh! it will be so nice," said she to he, "to keep a pretty cow, and then I can get up—when I have learned to milk—every morning and milk it; and when I put it" (the milk, not the cow) "in the churn, you can churn the butter while I drive the hens into the kitchen and make them lay their eggs, so that we may have them new laid and fresh as the butter. Then just before breakfast is ready, my dear, I can run out and stir up the skylarks in the fields, so that they may keep on singing all the time we are enjoying the eggs just laid, and the butter just churned."

But I digress. Mr. Herring furnished the champagne and Angelica, and I the boned turkey and other toothsome viands and *et-cæteras*. I laid the table, a good sized fall-leaf, in my room, but arranged the bridal-bower and bell in Delilah's part of the "Dovery." No one was invited but Mr. Wimple and Ben Butler. Ben Butler belonged to the "fat" Philistine across the street, Rosin Street. There was nothing very remarkable about the cat—it was a cat—unless it was a cast in one ear—cast down, which gave him a rakish, devil-may-care sort of expression quite foreign to his true character, I am certain, for he was very sedate and patriarchal in his deportment. He was a regular calling acquaintance of some of the members of my household; therefore I thought it no more than good manners dictated to invite him to act as third groomsman with Sally as third bridesmaid. Bismarck, Nellie's gallant, was second groomsman.

Sally wore a white demi-train, tarlatan dress, which was made—the demi—an inch longer than the tip end of her tail, which was black, and if the demi had not entirely covered it, Sally's *tout ensemble* would have been somewhat marred. I had everything ready, to exclaim as did the successful shipbuilder:

> "All is finished! and at length
>   Has come the bridal day
>   Of beauty and of strength;
> To-night the wedding guests are met!
> With sparkling gems the sky is set,
>   And o'er the bay,
> Slowly, in all her splendors dight,
> The great moon rises to behold the sight."

"What about Mr. Herring?" you ask. Well, nothing in particular. A bridegroom is a sort of necessary evil on such an occasion as this. You cannot get along without him, and you can hardly get along with him, and Mr. Herring was no exception to the rule. He wanted a room by himself, when there was none to be had. Whatever he wanted a room by himself for, I cannot imagine. It was too late to meditate upon his rashness, and he was all dressed but his gloves, and those he could put on in the piazza. However, I never allow a stoppage in the wheels I grease, and I soon had the doomed party standing in the bridal-bower directly under the bridal-bell, which was entirely made of white marguerettes with a calla lily for a clapper.

Bismarck and Nellie stood at the right of the groom; Bismarck in white favors and Nellie in blue tarlatan demi-train. I got blue for her dress, because Nellie is a mouse-colored black-and-tan, and blue and mouse blend so harmoniously that I could not afford to lose the effect. She wore a full wreath of orange-blossoms on her head, and a spray of hawthorn-buds on her breast. She was *first* bridesmaid, after all, for Mr. Wimple positively declined to stand up with the party who was to give away the bride. He said that no one could, with propriety, officiate in a double capacity at a wedding. Perhaps that was his only objection—perhaps? He might have understood me, I do not say that he did, but he might have remembered the old prophetic saw which says: "When the bell-wether scales the wall the sheep are sure to follow." There was nothing sheepish, however, about Mr. Wimple, he was more like dried calf. He played a part in the services, nevertheless, as witness, as he sat back on the lounge and alternately sucked the handle of his cane and twirled his eye-glass or the thumbs of his white kids, and smiled an approving smile. Ben Butler, in a white favor, also, held Sally by the paw, and looked majestically on. Sally showed to great advantage, charming young widow that she was. *Young* widows are always charming. Orange blossoms were upon brow and breast, and her yellow eyes looked very tender. The snuffy spot on her

MR. WIMPLE.

nose I had covered with *crême de lis;* and her tarlatan demi was properly held out by a camel-bustle.

"But do tell us about the bride!" Well, she looked charming, as all brides always do. The gray silk with a pink tinge was most becoming, and I would have my way and dust up her face with lily-white and a dash of rouge on her cheeks. A few hawthorn buds and blossoms gleamed among the dark braids of hair, which did not show the sprinkle of gray by gas-light, that adorned her shapely head. Some of the same flowers mingled with a knot of lace at her throat, and these were the only ornaments she indulged in, save a meek and lowly spirit. She was meek because she could not help herself, for the reason, as I have said, I would have my own way about everything; and the lowly part? Well, the least said about that, in my way of thinking, the better. My experience has taught me, and experience is a good master with first-class credentials, that "lowly" with the most of the "*umble*" means quite the "*reverse*."

The Rev. Cream got along swimmingly, considering the loud responses of the groom and the stiff assents of the bride. He was somewhat embarrassed and got out of his bearings, when he came to that passage in the stereotyped prayer where a *pious* joiner prays that the youthful pair may multiply and replenish the earth. But a little cough come to his relief in the nick of time. One cannot over-estimate the value of a little cough.

Sally, and Nellie, and I, all wept at the proper place; but it had a damaging effect upon Sally's personal appearance, for in wiping away the tears, with a great flourish of lace handkerchief, it took off a part of the *crême*, leaving the end of her nose in streaks, which gave it the appearance of our national flag in miniature—and somewhat out of repair at that.

As there had been no time to prepare wedding garments for the kittens, they were not invited.

When we rose up from the bridal-feast, the night had lapsed into the "wee sma' oors," and as there was neither boat nor train to Sacramento at that time o' day, I turned the bridal-bower into a bridal-chamber, and soon all was quiet in the "Dovery." But anon the stillness was broken in upon by a full band of cat-musicians, serenading the bride and groom. It seems that Ben Butler was a leader of a band of vocal instruments, and that he and Sally had planned this pleasant surprise, but that the time had been too short to train the numerous voices into a perfect union of effort. At the first opening note I sprang out of bed and opened the blinds of my window. The entire piazza, terrace, fence, and all the eucalyptus trees were covered with cats, and each cat was singing to his own peculiar pitch. Ben Butler was slowly moving his baton (the femur of a turkey) up and down, but so lost in admiration of Sally, that the serenade had been a secondary thing to him, if he remembered it at all.

Sally stood sweetly smiling, in bridal white, the centre of an admiring throng. True she looked somewhat discomposed; her camel-bustle was as one-sided as those worn by matinee-going ladies often are; and her orange-blossom wreath hung in a *negligée* manner suspended from one ear; her tail, no longer concealed, was beating rapid time to the music. Bismarck was sitting lost in meditation upon a fence-post, while his white satin favor floated gracefully over his back.

I heard a window fly up in the bridal-chamber, and the next instant a dark object, which resembled a man's boot, sped through the air. There was an unearthly yell and the post was vacant, and a million cats poured in party-colored waves and billows down the terrace, over the fence, down the stairs, and into the street. I saw a white object on the topmost branch of the tallest blue-gum tree, and presently Sally came down denuded of all her wedding "fixins," plain, simple Sally, on all fours. She called to her kittens that had taken shelter under the piazza, and when they came stealthily out of their hiding-place to meet her she kissed each one of them tenderly, and led the way to the box bedded with cotton cuttings.

Thus ends the history of cave life in a matrimonial scene. If any of my readers desire to know the wedded history of Delilah Hawthorn Herring they must learn it from her own lips. I never pry into skeleton closets.

Suffice it to say we parted in peace, Eben in slippers, and Delilah in tears. I blessed them and they blessed me, and thus the matter rests for the time being. The consistency of this chronicle of beautiful Probate life consists in its inconsistency, of broken detail, and kaleidoscopic pictures. The shifting scenery is in strict harmony with the *modus operandi* of beautiful Probate, however. In it I have been schooled and graduated, and the pupil's ways and deeds necessarily smack of the master's.

SCENE THE SEVENTH.

SEQUEL TO THE "HISTORY OF A PET DOG."

Fidelis ad urnam.

To those who have read "Probate Confiscation" *Jack* will be a familiar spirit. And having made his bow to *this* audience, you are not strangers. They will remember how *Justice*, with bandaged eyes searched for him, in behalf of an Esculapian— whom the thunderbolts avoid—throughout the highways and byways of San Francisco. How the Chinese quarter was ransacked, and hidden and unsavory things brought to light; how, during the search, no woman accompanied by a black and tan, or a pup of any sort on *four* legs, was safe from being pursued by private detectives, sheriffs, deputies and petty spies; how Esculapius whistled for days on street corners and public plazas — but whistled in vain, because the object of the whistle was carefully housed by admiring friends over the bay; how, after all stratagems failed, I was sued for the dog, and pugnaciously put in a defence. Perhaps they will be amused, I will take it for granted that they will be, at the following graphic history of the case which appeared at the time, in the *San Francisco Chronicle*, a daily paper which

JACK.

has been mentioned before in these pages; a paper on whose fearless face the sun, moon, and stars never set; a paper that employs no "pill mixer," and owns no cemetery lot.

VICISSITUDES OF A BLACK AND TAN'S LIFE.

From the Stable to the Parlor—efforts to deprive a lady of her pet —Mrs. Stow's opinion.

In Justice Joachimsen's Court yesterday the case of F. L. Howard vs. Marietta L. B. Stow, for the possession of a dog, occupied the greater part of the morning. The facts of the case are as follows: About six years ago J. W. Stow purchased a black and tan English terrier of a stableman for $5, thinking that he saw points in the "purp" rather superior to the ordinary canine rat-traps. The only failing the dog had was a violent antipathy to his brethren of the Newfoundland persuasion, whom he never hesitated to attack, regardless of the popular opinion that "the better part of valor is discretion." This was probably the result of the pernicious influence of the stable life from which he was rescued none too soon. His belligerent propensities got him into trouble after a while, and he was severely injured in an injudicious attempt to eat a dog several hundred times bigger than himself. Great was the sorrow thereat in the house of Stow, and for many days it was nip and tuck between the wounded pup and the grim destroyer, with a strong probability that tuck would get the best of it. A couch was prepared by loving hands, and everything done that humanity and the neighbors could suggest. Poultices, plasters, noxious draughts, patent medicines and all the other tortures that are heaped upon sick and helpless mankind were applied without stint to his dogship, while the servants and all the inmates of the house were kept in constant attendance upon his wants. "Oft in the stilly night" an agonizing howl would arouse every one within two blocks, and when the alarmed people of the house rushed to his assistance, it would be found that he wanted to turn over. This operation being conducted to the entire satisfaction of every one, the household would again wander off into dreamland, only to be ruthlessly recalled by an unearthly yelp, when Jack wanted his nose scratched. He would call the whole family up from the supper-table sometimes just to get some one to wag his tail for him. Thus it will be seen that the dog was quite a care, and when Mrs. Stow complained of the trouble she was put to on his account, her husband gave her the dog in part payment for her services, saying that when she got tired of him, she might give him to Dr. Howard. In due course of time Jack recovered, and became greatly attached to Mrs. Stow, and as his education progressed he renounced his low-bred stable ways, and became a high-toned dog. But alas! the hour of parting came, and the two friends were separated by many a weary mile of railroad and ocean. Mrs. Stow went to Europe, and while she was away her husband died, leaving the dog, as is alleged, to Dr. Howard. The thought of Jack being in strange hands so preyed upon Mrs. Stow, when the news reached her, that she packed up her trunks, bandboxes, and other *impedimenta*, and came home. Hearing that Jack was in Los Angeles, she repaired thither and hunted up Dr. Howard's ranch. The disciple of Esculapius was off somewhere making ante-mortem experiments on some unfortunate's internal anatomy, prior to turning him over to the undertaker; but his wife produced poor Jack at Mrs. Stow's request, and gave him up. What a wreck of a once noble doghood was there! The sleek and shiny coat, that once was carefully groomed every day, bore a striking resemblance to a worn-out door-mat, and moreover was thickly inhabited by the wicked and pestiferous flea. The general appearance of Jack was strongly suggestive of his having been dipped in the ash-barrel and run through a clothes-wringer tail foremost. A life of degradation and misery had been his lot after leaving the abode of pampered luxury where four happy years had been spent. Many a night had he gone to sleep and "dreamt he dwelt in marble halls," only to awake to the stern reality that he was under the back steps, and that an able-bodied flea had taken up a position on the back of his neck, from which it was difficult to dislodge him. Then he would get up and howl in the agony of his canine soul, endeavoring to thus relieve his troubled breast, and wipe away the sad recollections of the past in tears. But even this poor consolation was denied him, and an unsympathetic bootjack would generally punctuate his lamentations with a period. He found it was no use to mourn and fret about his altered condition in life, and he finally learned that the best thing he could do was to stand on his head in the corner and dissemble. Such was the life from which Jack was rescued by his loving mistress, who made allowance for the neglect shown him, on the ground that Mrs. Howard had three babies to wash, dress and powder, and having a mistaken idea that they were of more importance than the dog, had not bestowed the care upon him that his delicate nature required. Poor Jack wagged his tail nearly off the hinges when he found that he was going home.

The first thing done on the arrival of the train in San Francisco was to put Jack through a Turkish bath and reduce him to a state of semi-respectability. Under the fostering care beStow-ed upon him, he soon began to recover his natural appearance and lively disposition, the only mark of his vagabond life remaining being the involuntary drooping of both extremities at the raising of a hand above him. But let us return to

Los Angeles, and see how the representative of the noble house of Howard liked the confiscation of his live stock. With a portentous frown he made a break for the menial who had charge of the kennels, on his return home, and made some inquiries about the missing dog. "How now, caitiff! hast disposed of the canine for filthy lucre?" he thundered. The trembling vassal bowed low and said, "I hast not, me lud." With muttered curses deep the haughty pill-mixer strode toward the castle. 'Tis best to draw a vail over the rest of this chapter, or refer the reader to the Waverley novels for the proper scene and high-toned language usually used in such cases. The result was that the doctor hied him to 'Frisco with the firm determination to get that dog if he had to steal him. He wrote to Mrs. Stow, requesting her to send Jack to him, and received a note in return asking him to call on her. For some reason or other he did not pay her a visit, probably because he didn't want a lecture on the sins and general corruptness of the Probate Court. He sent a man after the dog, however, and the man didn't get him, but came away a raving maniac, talking incoherently about citations, letters of administration, mortmain, etc. The doctor then obtained a writ of replevin and sent the Sheriff to serve it; but the Sheriff didn't make a very astonishing success of it. He got into the house and went to Mrs. Stow's room, but when he demanded admittance the lady clasped Jack in her arms and stepped upon the balcony, where she stood like Rebecca the Jewess, ready to step into the next house if he succeeded in opening the door. Having some delicacy about breaking into a lady's boudoir in search of a dog, the Sheriff went away empty-handed. Then the deputy sheriffs took a hand and made a brilliant failure of the job. They brought every kind and description of dog that ever was thought of to the wielder of the scalpel. They woke him up from dreams of peace to examine their captures, and pestered the poor man with dogs until his life became a burden to him, and he even wished that he were dead. One particularly smart deputy came around at two o'clock in the morning, and beat the devil's tattoo on the front door until the man of physic came down under the impression that the whole city had been taken suddenly sick in the night and required his valuable services immediately. He was thoroughly disgusted to find the sheriff holding a big, white bull dog, with one ear chewed off, and an abbreviated tail making abortive attempts to wag the rest of the animal. He explained to the deputy in pure Saxon that he had got the wrong dog and that he was an unmitigated ass, and made some allusions to the canine maternity of the officer.

THE WRONG DOG.

The deputy resented the insinuation with spirit and said, "Sic 'im." The result was that the dog carried off about a yard of cotton night-shirt as a trophy. The next officer hunted around after Jack unsuccessfully for a day or two, and finally conceived a luminous idea, which he put into immediate execution. He took all the dogs from the Pound and corralled the whole herd in the Doctor's back yard, intending to come around in the evening and help him pick out Jack. He was so tickled with the idea that he went off and treated himself until he got gloriously drunk, and forgot all about the dogs. The Doctor got home late and went to bed. He got up pretty soon and began to fire the furniture into the back yard, beginning with bottles of hair oil, and finishing off with the stove. The only survivor of the bombardment was a poor little cross-eyed Scotch terrier, that looked as if he had been used as a foot-ball by a gang of hoodlums. He was too miserable to kill, and too tough to die of his own accord; so the doctor adopted him and called him Gavroche. But that hasn't got anything to do with Jack, who continued to elude the vigilant officers and detectives set upon the track. A CHRONICLE reporter detailed to look it up obtained the above story from Mrs. Stow. In the course of an interview before the trial Mrs. Stow said: "Cannot I get an offset, a kind of rebuttal, against the two hundred and fifty dollars claimed by Howard by bringing in a claim for services rendered as sick nurse? I have paid twenty dollars a week for nursing, not within the last two years, however; for when I was sick the Probate Judge would not allow me one extra sixpence for medical attendance. There is no encouragement held out to Probate widows to be interesting invalids; they must keep in robust health, or suffer for it. Two years ago Dr. Howard came here from Los Angeles to counsel with the attending physicians. He arrived on Friday, and on Tuesday following my husband died. Howard charged five hundred dollars for the visit. That ought to have paid him for his services, without wanting my dog, when I have lost all but it and the spot where my husband is buried. I am sued for the dog, and they have asked me to set a price upon the bones of my husband

and the few feet of earth surrounding them, and a small price at that. Where am I to be hidden if I sell my only inheritance for a few pieces of money, and what shall I do with the money? Save it for cremation, or buy a 'love of a bonnet?' Who has the best right to Jack, Dr. Howard or I? I have possession of him and possession is nine points of law."

After a patient hearing of the case Justice Joachimsen or-

ESCULAPIUS.

dered that "the dog Jack be returned to the plaintiff, or the defendant pay five dollars in lieu thereof, together with the costs of the court, amounting to twelve dollars."

This case was not tried in beautiful Probate, because beautiful Probate is not a criminal (?) court, and I was amenable to the laws of a criminal court for unlawfully getting possession of my dog, the same as though I had unlawfully got possession of my child, that beautiful Probate had playfully taken from me. This criminal court could have imprisoned me for not producing the body of Jack in court, if the contestant had insisted upon it, the same as beautiful Probate could imprison me for unlawfully getting possession of my own flesh and blood, in the person of my child, and then refusing to bring it into court. But Esculapius, unlike Probate, was too amiable and tender-hearted to carry his masculine power to the extreme tether of the law.

When the contestant and his downy-lipped attorney and the great cloud of antagonistic witnesses had departed out of the court-room, I thanked the judge for his kindness in setting so *small* a price on the head of Jack, and going down-stairs to the clerk's office, I then and there deposited the sum of seventeen dollars, the combined costs of court and the judge's estimated value of the dog.

Three or four months later I called at the clerk's office to learn if the court's decision had been accepted by the belligerents, and the money taken. The polite court official informed me that it had not been accepted, and further said, "Mrs. Stow, you had better take your gold, they will never come to a moneyed settlement, for they are bent on having the dog." Then he handed me a little sealed package, and on opening it I discovered my seventeen dollars. Taking out five I handed the twelve back to him. "Keep it all," he said, "and let the court collect the costs, which it will be very unlikely to do."

Fearing that I might further offend the dignity of the law and break the peace, without the sanction of higher authority, I proceeded in a body (of one) upstairs and got the "all right" from his "Honor" the judge; the why and the wherefore will remain one of the unsolved problems in my court experience forever.

For more than a year after the trial, Jack lived in peace with all the world, with the exception of gophers and ground squirrels, at my sister's home in Oakland. But the astute vigilantees at last got scent of his whereabouts, and one day when she was shopping in San Francisco, the alert Esculapius made a grand sortie upon the unguarded outposts and captured poor Jack without firing a gun.

When the "Heathen-Chinee" gardener saw the playful and *manly* transaction, he flew to the rescue with braided cue streaming in a parallel line behind his head as he frantically brandished the rake he held in his hands, and cried: "Drop dog! drop dog!" and when the "pill-mixer" refused to "drop dog" the infuriated Heathen laid the rake vigorously about the ears and back of the invader, who made a precipitate retreat, and taking leg-bail he was soon inside a street car, with the determined Chinaman blowing a policeman's whistle, in hot chase.

The latter sprang upon the platform, gesticulating and filling the air with celestial oaths, as he showered maledictions thick and fast on the head of the offender.

Passing the upbound car, the sharp-eyed Mongolian saw my sister inside of it, on her way home, and leaping from one platform to the other, shouted, "Man, car, Jack! man, car, Jack! Belly bad man, belly bad, gottee Jack. Me plentee fytee he; no fytee he me. Me, blow, blow, blow, hap hour, no fliceman come; bym by fliceman he come, too muchee late, man catch Jack and lun away; fliceman no catchee him."

Sister Gertie took in the situation at a glance, and stopping her car prepared to enter the other; but the quondam doctor preferred to have it out without witnesses, and so betook himself and Jack to the sidewalk, where there was a hasty but polite exchange of opinions upon the subject of ownership, etc. Then the aggrieved possessor said:

"I shall never recover from the punishment inflicted by your heathen gardener. My lumbar region is permanently injured by the blows from the rake, and I fear that enlargement of the heart will ensue from fright; for, having Jack in my arms, I could not parry the blows;" saying which, he tied a string to poor Jack's collar and led him triumphantly away.

When the dog realized that he was being taken from my sister, he turned with a look of astonishment and reproach upon his countenance, which said plainer than words, "Have I ever betrayed your confidence or forsaken you? Have I not given measure for measure in sincere affection and honest watchfulness for all I have received at your hands?"

So the old fellow was taken back to the Esculapian abode in Los Angeles, to be the companion of preserved reptiles and fishes, tadpoles and alligators; trilobites and leviathans; lizards and extinct saurians; of skeletons of parallelopipedons—no, I mean of palæotheriums; of retorts and condensers; of jars (not family) of liquids and innumerable gases; and of huge specimens of his master's primitive ancestry. He was again to be the companion of an ever-increasing houseful of children (the name of Howard is not likely to become extinct this generation); to watch the cats in the orange groves, and to create consternation among Freeman's rodents.

Thus ends the second chapter on the life, character, adventures, and vicissitudes of a much-valued friend—*a dog*. His former noble-hearted master, J. W. Stow, loved him very much, and said to me often, "Lizzie, if Jack outlives me, I wish when he is dead you would have him buried at my feet." This I most solemnly promised to do, and when the breath is out of the "*body*," which interested parties so much desired to have produced in court, I should like to keep the pledge made to my husband, and put the faithful creature under the sod—forever out of the reach of contestation—at the feet of his master.

SCENE THE EIGHTH.

SEASONABLE ADVICE TO WIDOWS.

Acriora orexim excitant embammata.

THESE receipts are given solely for the benefit of that large class of—well, *fortunates*, that are daily, hourly, momentarily, expecting distribution of colossal estates, and while living in expectancy *may be*, I do not say that they will be, somewhat puzzled to know just how to keep soul and body together, as expectancy does not fill the stomach, nor cover the back.

All outsiders—I mean by this, all such as are not enfolded in beautiful Probate's motherly bosom, or better still, *fatherly* bosom—all such are warned and cautioned against reading the following receipts, and much more are forbidden to make practical use of knowledge thus surreptitiously and unlawfully obtained, without the full concurrence and *written* consent of the author. I am a humane humanitarian, and were I to suffer the world at large to use these receipts, what, pray, would be the result of the indiscretion? What? All provision dealers and butchers, and market-men, would go frantically into bankruptcy, and thus there would be thrown upon society at large, a very great respectable pauper class. The times would become thoroughly demoralized; every joint out of kilter; every screw loose; every rivet flawed; every nail rusted; every spike twisted; every bolt bent; every band "*busted;*" every tie broken. You see the risk I run, but I feel that I can place entire confidence in a conservative public. Were I, for an instant, to doubt their good faith, these invaluable recipes for widows would be cast to the flames at once, *for I am discreet.*

My subject is such a pregnant one, that I scarcely know where to begin. However, dear sister Probate widows, I expect we are all about the same in our style of living, tucked away like spinning spiders, in by-corners and unused cubby-holes; therefore, you must not feel that I am egotistical if I draw largely upon my individual experience. Bear with me, and also bear in mind that practical knowledge is better than "book larnin'."

These are winter recipes, which with a little

variation will answer for summer. Do not let the season chosen cause any coolness between us. This time of the year is taken because everything is much dearer in winter than in summer, and therefore one is obliged to economize much closer, to live on a small allowance or a slender income. With these preliminary remarks, I think I may safely begin to handle my subject without gloves.

Firstly, then, I will suppose that your cooking utensils and dishes are a bowl, a good sized one, a cup and saucer, and a knife, a carving-knife. It is better to have a carving-knife on many accounts. In moments of peril it answers the purpose of a short sword, a battle-axe, a poniard, a cleaver, or spear; and for domestic purposes it is the knife of knives. With it you can carve up your old leather boots for slipper soles (all Probate widows should understand the art of making their own slippers, for "boughten" slippers cost money); pare, and slice, and chop up all sorts of vegetables, split up boxes and your landlady's latticed arbor for kindling wood, with the aid of a dumb-bell. No Probate widow should be without dumb-bells for a moment. They are positively invaluable. Besides their efficacy in promoting health and physical development, they serve as the innocent tack-hammer, or the murderous battering-ram and catapult. Now we have got as far as the fork—a two-pronged old-fashioned steel one. I make choice of this kind or style of fork, because it is handier for making toast, broiling a rasher or squab, and for fastening down the window to keep out burglars, or to untie your shoestring or corset-string, or apron string, or night-cap string, or a difficult question, or a hard knot of any kind. If it is a good tempered fork you can punch the holes in your slipper soles with it, in conjunction with a dumbbell, and thus save the price of a cobbler's awl.

Almost every provident landlady provides one small tumbler—which small tumbler originally contained gelatine flavored with currant, pineapple, or raspberry—for drinking purposes; for medicinal concoctions; for a tooth-mug and to mix flour paste in— a sticky substance which takes the place of mucilage with Probate widows.

Now we have come to the teaspoon. A teaspoon is another indispensable utensil—a silver-plated one. It is better and safer on many accounts to have a silver-plated than a Simon Pure. It does not bend so easily when you are scraping the burnt apple-sauce off the bottom of the skillet, and should it play the coquette by getting up a clandestine flirtation with your "chinee" chambermaid and elope with him some fine morning, it would not break your heart or prove an irreparable loss. A teaspoon is one of the handiest things in the world. There is not an hour in the day but you feel the need of a teaspoon. My satchel never goes anywhere without a teaspoon inside of it, and my satchel never goes anywhere without me outside of it. I never lend my satchel, and I never lend my teaspoon. A satchel is another indispensable thing for a Probate widow. In fact, a Probate widow would not be *ex cathedrâ* without a satchel. But how I do run away from the spoon! The teaspoon which I use many, many times every day of my life, I have used every day for the last five years—all my years of Probate probation so far. It went to Europe with me before I was a Probate widow, and it returned with me after I was a Probate widow. It accompanied me and my bill to Sacramento in '76; it journeyed to Oregon, and to Los Angeles and Santa Barbara with me and my satchel.

THE PERAMBULATING SATCHEL.

THE LITTLE SILVER-PLATED.

Ah! what an obedient servant that teaspoon has been, and still is. What a medium it has been—and still is—between dish and mouth. I should be lost without that teaspoon, and that teaspoon would be lost without me.

Secondly, you *must* have a tin pint cup—no, a pint tin cup—no, a pint of cup tin—no, well, never mind! so it holds a pint. You will have to have a spirit-lamp to heat, cook, or warm whatever is in the little pint cup. I bought mine, together with the little pint tin cup, in Paris, and paid three francs for them. I do not mention this fact because I set up my little tin pint cup as a monopoly of little pint tin cups, for American tin is quite equal to French tin, and American brass is quite equal to French brass. But, as I was saying, no Probate widow can dispense with a little tin pint cup for a day. The things she can make in it, tea and coffee, and chocolate, and hot milk, and hot water, and hot lemonade with a stick in it, and mulled claret, and mulled cider, and mulled beer and every and all other hot drinks used as beverages and thirst quenchers—mulled or otherwise. And then if she is sick she can make all kinds of hot "*yarb* drinks" in it—boiled catnip and dogwood; coltsfoot and lady's slipper; camomile and cumfrey; motherwort and bachelor-button; tanzy and tarweed; witch-hazel and hazel without the witch; and all and every other kind of herb and blossom known to the pharmacopœia.

And, dear a me! what cannot be done in a little pint cup in the way of cooking edibles! Every vegetable, root, head, leaf or branch known to the kingdom, can be boiled in it; all kinds of soups, stews, hash and meats can be made and cooked in it; all kinds of boiled puddings, excepting English plum, can be boiled in it.

Thirdly, *The skillet*, whose price is above rubies, if we take into account its various and sundry uses. It must have a cover and a handle. No skillet is complete and worthy the name of skillet without a cover and a handle. A friend of mine—a Probate widow friend—had a skillet, but the cover was lost and the handle broken off, so that she was always obliged to handle it, when hot, with the tongs. It had a remarkable appearance— that skillet had. It was not a handsome utensil, and on that account it should have been well behaved; but it was not. One day when I was invited to lunch with my friend she was making the chocolate in it, when, without an instant's warning, it viciously turned over on its side and all the chocolate poured out over

THE VICIOUS SKILLET.

the coals and left us with nothing to drink, and made the room smell like a gas house, and put out all the fire. If the skillet is lined with porcelain (every Probate widow's skillet should be lined with porcelain) she can boil her handkerchiefs, and heat water for lavatory purposes in it, besides its innumerable uses in the culinary department. There are very few things in the boiling line but that you can boil in a skillet; there are very few things in the stewing line but that you can stew in a skillet; and there are but very few things in a fricasseeing line but that you can fricassee in a skillet.

Then there is the shovel. A shovel is not usually considered to be a cooking utensil, but that is an oversight that must not be passed over. A shovel in the hands of an adept—and I take it that all Probate widows *are* adepts—can be made much of. The handle of mine was loose, off, in fact, and at first I was inclined to complain; but I soon learned to rejoice greatly that the handle could be placed and displaced at pleasure. When I was boiling a dinner in my skillet, " skillet luck," I laid the shovel, after carefully removing the handle, over the coals in my open grate (every Probate widow should have a stove with an open grate to it), in order to conserve the heat that would else have escaped up the chimney, and been diffused in general warmth for the benefit of the city instead of boiling my "luck"; it—the shovel on the coals—in this manner made a firm rest for the inside of the skillet—no, for the outside of the inside of the skillet—no, I mean for that portion of the skillet which rested upon the inverted shovel in the stove. I often cooked my entire dinner on that shovel. It would take a magician to compute the number of steaks, chops, cutlets, soles, rashers, oysters and clams that I have fried, broiled, and deviled on that shovel; the ham and eggs, and sausages, and potatoes—sweet and otherwise—that I have eaten hot from its smoking and fragrant surface; the mustard plasters that I have warmed on it; the little strip of red flannel dipped in salt diluted with vinegar—a sovereign cure for sore throat and Probate qualms—which has so often steamed upon it, ere it was placed about the "stiff neck" for the night. This most valuable concocted dilution—salt and vinegar—was usually heated in the little pint tin cup, but when the little pint tin cup was washed and laid up in ordinary for the night, I often found it necessary to augment caloric in the little red flannel

THE CONVENIENT SHOVEL.

band, by laying it tenderly, for a brief period, upon the hot shovel.

Fourthly—having described a Probate widow's cooking utensils—we will now, if you please, take up the food which is to be cooked in them, in order. Breakfast, with a Probate widow, is, in reality, a very simple thing. A bit of dry toast and tea, perhaps served on last evening's *Post*, in lieu of spotless damask—but in imagination it is magnificent. Fit for a king or queen, even. While she craunches the dry toast, and drinks the tea without any milk in it (I never took milk excepting when I lived in the Cave. Milkmen do not, as a rule, serve milk to attic tenants), her imagination runs riot among toothsome viands. Tender steaks, garnished with parsley; broiled partridge; quail on toast; lamb chops in caps; cutlets in frills; and if an acquaintance be sharing the feast, a mutual friend or two, " broiled, scored and deviled," and served hot, makes an admirable relish. It gives an edge to the tongue, as well as the appetite.

Lunch is too trivial to mention. The larger portion of Probate widows, I presume, dispense with it altogether, or are of a disinterested and generous turn of mind, and drop in upon an acquaintance about the time of day that lunches are in order.

Then, again, an attractive Probate widow is often invited to lunch with a gentleman friend, at the *Maison Doré*, on his wife's reception day. It appears to be more convenient for the friend that day.

But the dinner is the meal which brings out the masterly ability, the hidden resources, the cunning devices, the crowning glory of a Probate widow's culinary skill. She must set her wits to work if she would achieve a brilliant success by the rubbing together of two sticks, in order to make a feast. But it can be done, as I shall demonstrate ere I close this chapter. You can almost call such a dinner a "*wit dinner*," as so much depends upon the activity of the brain. Torpidity, in any form, is death to Probate widows. They must be as sharp-eyed as a hawk; as far-seeing as an eagle; as wise as an owl; as swift-footed as the mountain roe; as industrious as the honey bee; as wary as the fox; and they must be *patient* withal—as patient as the waves of the sea, that never tire of climbing, climbing, that never weary of receding, receding.

But, let me see! where am I? where did I leave off? Ah! at the dinner. I surmised as much. Well, in the first course comes the soup. Some kinds of soup, manufactured by Probate widows, has to be almost entirely made out of "*stock*," which is constantly kept in a cool place, tightly corked and bottled, to prevent evaporation. A Probate widow's stock she always keeps in her head, because a Probate widow always observes the golden rule, "head cool, feet hot" (excepting at dinner), therefore she has a liberal supply of *imaginative soup* on hand at all times, which is called, in Probate parlance, "Imaginative stock."

So much for preliminaries, now let us commence. Put a small handful of rice into the little pint cup— a very *small* handful— for rice to a novitiate is the most unreliable edible in the world. I put a large handful into my little tin pint cup, and lighting the little spirit furnace underneath it, I felt at rest and peace with the whole world, and the little tin pint, and the rice and water—Spring Valley water—in it, and the little French fiery furnace under it. But in a few moments I was startled out of my peaceful mood, by a mizzling, and a fizzling, and a

THE LITTLE FIERY FURNACE.

sizzling, and looking in the direction of the little fiery furnace, brooded over by the little tin pint cup, with the rice and the nutritious Spring Valley in it, I was greatly amazed to see a full-blown poppy popping out of the top of the little pint cup, in the form of a rice blossom. I had left off the cover of the little pint tin cup in order to skim the Spring Valley when it should boil, little dreaming of the deceitful properties of rice.

Therefore, I most emphatically say in this rice soup recipe that Probate widows must use only a very small amount of rice. When it is thoroughly done—on no account let it boil long enough to have a grain broken—lift a part of it out for dessert. Salt this portion and lay a small piece of butter and a little bit of apple sauce, or gooseberry jam, or tart jelly in the centre of the rice. You had better dig a little well in the middle, or sink a shaft by the aid of your silver-plated teaspoon, and into the well or shaft drop the jam, or sauce, or jelly and the little piece of butter, and over all sprinkle a pinch or two of sugar—you will find, when you come to eat it, a charming pudding. To keep it warm—it is better warm than cold—put it beside the fiery furnace, or, better still, set it on the stove-hearth. Pour into the remainder of the rice and the boiling liquor in the little tin pint cup a generous amount of "Imaginative Stock." You had better use the chicken imaginative for rice soup. However, some people prefer their stock to be composed of all and every kind of meat; this adapts it to all and every kind of soup, and gravies, and stuffing. At this stage of the soup's progress you must drop in a little dab of salt, and a little pepper dab, and sweet "*yarb*" to your taste.

After you have partaken of the soup you must perform some lively feats of imagination by the aid of vigorous thought. This is the next course in order. Think about fish, soft crabs, lobsters, eels, oysters, scollops and all kinds of shell fish, and fish without shells. Think how they taste boiled, roasted, fried, broiled; think how a speckled trout would taste after he had lain in hot ashes beside a stump camp-fire long enough to be done to a turn; think of a picnic of two on a shady bank along with such things as a—well, such things as go to make a substantial basket for out-of-door appetites; think of the blue sky above your head, the running river at your feet, and the yellow sunlight over all.

Now comes the roast. It looks strangely for a roast, I admit; but nevertheless it *is* a roast. It was in a down-town restaurant oven yesterday, or the day before. But you were obliged to heat it up in the skillet, along with the sweet potato which you brought home in your pullback pocket. It tastes good, for there are several things in it that were not in the plain roast yesterday, or the day before. There is a little Spring Valley water in it, and a little "Stock Imaginative," and a little dash of sweet herbs, and a little dab of butter; and it has been well stirred with the little silver-plated. That of itself, if you are a homœopathist, adds much to the strength and efficacy of the compound—as a nourisher.

Dinde aux truffle is the next course. Your *dinde* must be an imaginative *dinde*. But then, if you are anything of an idealist, you can manufacture a beautiful bird, by the aid of your mind's eye, and nothing surpasses an ideal. The ideal hero, lover, or friend, even, is far more captivating than a flesh and blood hero, lover, or friend; and I see no reason why an ideal turkey and mushrooms might not be as much above and beyond a real, feathered turkey and succulent mushrooms, as a beautiful thought is above and beyond the actual transaction, the real ponderable substance of form, and color, and weight. The only difference, as it appears to me, is, that one is etherialized, and the other is materialized. One is the feast of the mind and flow of imagination, while the other is a purely sensuous enjoyment.

The next course is the charming pudding, with its butter and jelly shaft, or well, in the centre. It is well, eat it! I say nothing about vegetables, because they do not rise into the realm of imagination.

Now comes the crowning effort. The grand finale, the last course. Bread, *pâte de foie gras*, cheese, fruit, champagne (you see I am something of an epicure), nuts, raisins, oranges, confectionery, cognac and black coffee. These, of course, are all etherial productions, but they are enjoyable and do not cause dyspepsia nor a pain in the head the next morning, and the expense of soda water.

You had better sit close up to the stove while you are enjoying your dinner—that is if you suffer with cold feet, which you are very likely to do, at dinner, owing to the heavy draft upon your imaginative faculties. But a new difficulty presents itself— your table is under hospital treatment. One leg having been dislocated by the careless expressman when he was bringing it upstairs. It stands up bravely when it can lean against the wall, but to venture to move it would be destruction; therefore, you must eat on your superfluous chair; and if it will not hold all the good things, make a sideboard of the floor under it. Your bread and gingerbread you can stand on end against the round which has not gone to kindle the fire yet, and if your cat—providing you have one—or dog, with the same provision, smells of the bread and gingerbread, what matter? He, or they, will not eat it so long as the savory flavor of meat and soup is in their noses.

When I resided in the cave with the seven cats, they were always greatly exercised the moment I commenced getting my dinner. Bismarck would climb atop of the stove (truth), it was not a high one, and as it is not very cold in San Francisco, and coals are somewhat dear, it was never very hot. The others were more patient. Sally was a pink of propriety. She rarely ever begged, and never for herself, but, if the kittens were very hungry, she was eloquent in her appeal on their behalf. I have seen many mothers, but I never saw a more devoted one than Sally Mouses. She would sit in the midst of milk and meat and not touch a particle of anything until her little ones were satisfied, and she would cuff Bismarck right and left when he got more than his share. It was very amusing to see the five kittens sitting in a row, with their paws folded, waiting while Sally kept guard over them, with Bismarck perched on the stove.

All Probate widows should keep themselves in splendid physical repair, for they are liable to get sadly out at the elbows and toes, fabrico-materially, during probate probation. Still they may stumble into Pandora's realm unconsciously. I put my foot in it, my right foot, which I found too late, was all *wrong*. At one time it became quite unmanageable, in fact, and when I insisted upon its accompanying me down-town to assist at the sale of *Probate Confiscation*, it would start obedient enough, but with malice aforethought and on mischief bent; for just as I had got well into a business frame of mind, that right-*wrong*-foot would insist upon going home and having a Turkish bath in—well, in hot salt and Spring Valley, and afterwards being wrapt up in lamb's wool, or cotton-batting, or old flannel, or being put into a warm stocking and old slipper. All of which was very inconvenient for me. I reasoned with that foot, but unlike its owner it was perfectly unreasonable. Then I paid a visit to a famous French chiropodist, and besought his aid. Said he, without examining the refractory member:

"Vat is ze matair vid ze foot? Ze korn, madame?"

"Corn and *contrariness!*" I replied, as I mentally and ruefully counted the unsold books in my invisible pockets.

"Vat you meenz by ze *kontrairinaiz?* Ze goo'? I am not ze doctair for ze goo', madame."

"But I have not got the gout," I said; "that's a man's disease. A woman rarely has the gout and a Probate widow is the last person in the world to be afflicted with a high-living complaint. It surely cannot be that."

"*Excusez-moi*, madame" (with a shrug of the shoulders and an elevation of the eyebrows), "but vat do you manger—eat—for ze breakfast?"

"Partridge on toast, quail on toast, duck on toast, hot rolls and pâte de foie gras, and tomatoes, pickles, and preserves," I replied with unfeigned surprise that such a polite practitioner should seek to pry into *cuisine*, after a remedy for a sore toe.

"Mon Dieu! mon Dieu! madame, zat brings ze goo' certain-mong, madame. You stopz ze partrage, ze quail and ze leetle duck, and manger only ze tea and ze toast dry *pour le* breakfast, madame, nozing more. Vat you have *pour le diner*, madame?"

Wondering more and more, I made answer: "Soup, fish, roast beef, *dinde aux trauffle*, chicken, and salad—"

"*Diable! Mon Dieu!* madame, zat is enough" (holding up his hands), "you tells me no more.

You live too *way up*. You no more manger zoze tings, eat *le bœuf*—vat you calls him?"

"Rare," I suggested. "Wee madame, le bœuf raire, *va-rie* raire, madame, and one leetle pomme de terre, and a leetle salad, and one leetle cheeken, and one leetle boutelle de vin rouge. Zat'll mend ze toze, madame, wizout ze medicin."

But bless my soul, how my degenerate foot has led me away from my text, "Recipes for Probate Widows." However, the dinner was finished, and there was nothing more to do but to shake the table-cloth (*Daily Post*), brush up the crumbs, wash the little silver-plated and hang up the skillet. Then comes the twilight frolic with the kits—and then—

.

> The work is done and the day is gone,
> And queenly Night asserts her throne,
> And Sleep bends down with a gentle kiss,
> Sealing the eyes in leathern bliss,
> Till we float in dreamland mystic, sweet,
> And in rainbow-seas we bathe our feet,
> Till pain is hushed in the healing wave,
> Till the heart leaps up from its living grave,
> To meet and to hold in a close embrace
> A truth that is truth in every place.

SCENE THE NINTH.

JANE GILPIN'S PROBATE ASS.

Quasi agnum committere lupo.

JANE GILPIN was a widow
  Of beauty and renown;
A Probate widow eke was she,
  Of famous 'Cisco town.

Jane Gilpin's husband "*John*" was dead,
  Which grieved her heart full sore,
And weeping sadly at his grave,
  Her fate she did deplore.

When left alone within her home
  A home so desolate—
Alas! the house was filled with gloom,
  Where Death had sat so late.

So late had sat in noble state,
  A sceptre in his hand,
Which every mortal bows before,
  The noble and the grand.

She wandered thro' the solemn rooms,
    But every object there
Was rife with haunting memories,
    The dirge note of despair.

She locked the doors, and closed the blinds,
    Then sat her down in grief,
And mourned that one so young as she
    Had happiness so brief.

She gathered to her stricken heart
    Her *pretty children* three—
Three handsome boys—so like her John;
    But where, O where was he?

"Hark! what is this I hear?" quoth Jane,
    "A voice comes from the town;
It bids me don my cloak and hat,
    And on the ass ride down.

The Probate Ass! Ah! woe is me!
    My heart is hot and sore.
How can I mount this Probate beast
    That's braying at my door?"

Jane Gilpin in her widow's weeds
    A picture was to see;
So lithe and girlish was her form;
    Her step so light and free.

The ass stood pawing at the gate
    So sleek, so fat, so strong,
For widow's gold was in his veins,
    His eyes were full of song.

He laughed outright in merry glee,
   And champed his silver bit,
The pretty widow for to see,
   And said, " This is a hit ! "

Ah ! widow's oats were in his skin
   And widow's corn and meal.
'Twas widow's silver in his mouth—
   And on his treacherous heel.

Jane Gilpin seated on his back
   Her tears fell down like rain ;
And then she spoke—" O gentle ass,
   My heart is rent in twain.

At parting with my lovely babes,
   My house, my cat, my dog ! "
Said he, " No cause for that, my dear ;
   Take every precious tog."

Smack went his lips, up went his heels,
   Was never ass so glad ;
The stones did rattle underneath
   As tho' Deathside were mad.

Jane Gilpin on the ass's back
   Seized fast the bristling mane,
And drew her darlings to her breast,
   In mortal fear and pain.

She felt the demon at her heart,
   A swooning death-like spasm,
And rousing, saw her babes afar—
   The ass had leaped a chasm.

With outstretched arms her darlings stood
    Upon a rocky ledge,
And pleading called, "O mamma dear,
    Come lift us o'er the edge."

A stern cold hand was on them laid,
    A cold command was given—
"Come right along!" This is the way
    That tender ties are riven.

This is the age—the Christian age
    Of manly strength and a'—
That tears the babe from mother's breast,
    Because it is the *law*.

"O cruel Probate Ass!" she cried,
    "What treachery is this?"
"Please calm yourself, my lady fair—
    You'll soon get used to this,"

The ass replied in dulcet notes,
    And skipped his heels about;
The exercise was sure to keep
    At bay the naughty gout.

"O spare my babes!" the mother cried,
    "Give me my darling sons,
No guardian like a mother's love,
    Can shield her little ones.

"O Ass, dear Ass, dear Probate Ass,
    On bended knee I pray—
God gave my precious children three,
    How dare you take away?"

Loud laughed the ass, and mocking cried,
  "Let *Him* protect you now!
Jane Gilpin, you are Probate plunder—
  A funny chit, I vow!"

With this he gave a snort like mad,
  And balanced on his toes,
And danced the wildest witch's dance,
  To the music of his nose.

Down came the house, down came the cat,
  Down came the poodle dog;
And then he tore along the road
  Like a demon all agog.

Away, away, went widow Jane
  Away went cloak and hat,
"Stop, stop!" she cries, "how dare you leave
  My treasure-trove like that?

"I'm starving, dying here alone,
  Give me my loved ones back;
Give me my babes, my lands, my house,
  My poodle dog, my cat."

But time sped on, and Jane grew old
  Upon the tireless ass;
O weary journey, long and sad
  For years and years, alas!

The Probate Ass had never flagged;
  Her hair was thin and white;
Deep furrows seemed her hollow cheeks,
  Her eyes had lost their light.

At last a dreary plain was reached,
    All sand and barren rock;
Up went the heels of Probate Ass,
    Down came Jane a-shock.

A cloud of dust was all she saw
    Except some fiery stars;
She cowered there alone, alone,
    Defaced by many scars.

And when the midnight moon arose
    It saw her lying there,
Dead, cold and dead, and turned to stone,
    An everlasting prayer,

That time nor change cannot destroy;
    A shrine for pilgrim feet,
Whose lips of stone most eloquent
    Shall plead in accents sweet:

That mercy, justice, love and peace
    May fall like heavenly dew;
Or thunder with a wrath divine;
    Do right, be brave, be true!

Give custom to the flame and sword
    Where wrong, in heated steel,
Is driven thro' the human heart,
    Despite the wild appeal,

That rings on every morning breeze,
    And echoes from the grave—
" Oh heed the right, Oh-spare the weak,
    And the downtrodden *save!* "

SCENE THE TENTH.

TABLES TURNED.

Dux femina facti.

Tableau: An open court, beautiful Probate, with the imposing and unapproachable judgess (a widow) enthroned upon the *bench;* in other and more correct phraseology, enthroned upon beautiful Probate's "revolver"—a scarlet revolver, padded and stuffed with votes—*female* votes—for every man has had his day. Behind this three-legged revolver—for it is an elevated concern mounted like a catapult, or battering-ram, or howitzer—is a scarlet canopy looped, and braided, and fringed, and buttoned like a fusileer, or grenadier, or any other Mogul or Moguless.

Her "*Honoress*" is an eloquent specimen of Anglo-Saxon womanhood, with a fine open brow, keen black eyes, thin nostrils, and a firm-set mouth. She is what is called "a fine woman," in the prime of life. Her dark glossy hair is worn in puffs about the forehead, and the soft braids at the back of the queenly-poised head are surmounted by a tortoise-shell comb from which depends a ripple of delicate lace, bearing in every fibre of its exquisite texture

THE JUDGESS.

the enviable tint of age. It falls back of the pearly ear, and floating downward in easy grace just reaches the velvet band encircling her white throat.

On the index finger of her left hand she wears a diamond solitaire of the purest water. Her black silk judicial gown is of the richest importation and faultless in its make and garniture. With a lively appreciation of her lofty position she presides with great ease and dignity of manner.

Ranged upon her right are the juryesses, twelve in number and all in gowns. On her left are the witnesses, a "great cloud," eager to testify; while immediately in front of her are seven learned counselloresses and their seven bags of blue briefs; no, their seven blue grief bags, no, their seven brief blue receptacles filled to bursting with legal documents concerning dead wives and live husbands and motherless children's estates. These blue bags, together with a countless number of law tomes, are lying upon the green baize table-cover before the seven noses of the seven learned counselloresses. Other members of the bar are scattered here and there, ready to put in an "appearance" for any absentee or minor child that has been overlooked, or that may chance to turn up.

As soon as the judgess on this particular occasion had formally opened the court, the clerkess (who also acted in the capacity of crieress, a little cricket of a woman, in short hair and round-bowed spectacles), with a great flourish of pen and paper, called the first case that appeared on the court calendar, which case was "Crape *vs.* Beautiful Probate."

For an instant after Mr. Crape was ordered into court there was a death-like silence; nothing was audible save the beating of the seven hearts of the seven learned counselloresses. Soon, however, there was a slight stir among the bystanders, who hung on the outskirts of the court like fringe on a petticoat, and then a small pale man, clad in the sables of grief, with a wart on his nose, and two yards and a half of bombazine depending from his hat-band, came slowly forward. He looked meek, and his deportment was mild, but one cannot always depend upon looks and appearance. Under the most suave exterior there may slumber a volcano.

"Judgess," he faltered, turning the hat in his hands until the bombazine appendage formed a little black pyramid of grief at his feet, "I desire to serve as one of the executors of the late lamented Mrs. Crape's will;" saying which he buried his face in a black handkerchief, as big as a blanket, with a small white spot in the centre, and sobbed aloud.

JUDGESS.—You were not appointed in the will, Mr. Crape, and therefore cannot act with the executoresses therein named.

"How *very* strange!" said Mr. Crape abstractedly.

"It is not at all strange," replied the judgess, with a slight touch of irony in her voice. "If you had been a proper and capable person to have administered upon the estate, you would not have been ignored. No one knows you as well as the late lamented Mrs. Crape did. She was better acquainted with your shortcomings than I am, and, therefore, was a better judge of your incapacity than I am. I shall respect her decision, sir, and there is no use in arguing the question; I shall not change my mind."

"But, yer Honoress," pleaded Mr. Crape, "I helped earn the property, and the laborer is worthy of his hire."

J. You were paid as you went, most likely, in food and clothes, in love and cigars, in having a house over your head and a bed under your back. At all events, *you* did not bear and rear the children, puke them in measles, catnip them in colds, smartweed them in croups, and blister them in fevers. You did not pinafore, roundabout, and surtout them during toddlehood; you did not sweet-oil their earache, poultice their burns, mend their knees and rag their many bleeding wounds; you did not quiet them, at midnight, with soothing syrup, "Mother Goose," and squills during the tortures of colic.

"I earned all the money that bought the squills," continued Mr. Crape, catching at the last straw.

"*What egotism!*" exclaimed the judgess in a low voice; at which the clerkess and the seven counselloresses turned up their seven + one learned noses and said, "*Did you ever?*"

"I repeat the assertion," continued the judgess, addressing Mr. Crape; "you were more than compensated every day and hour of your life by the love of wife and babes; by the sweet and sacred joys of home; you were clothed and fed, and all your buttons sewed on. What more could a reasonable man ask? Besides all these manifold blessings, you have your '*dower*' in Mrs. Crape's real estate."

"There is no real estate, and Mrs. Crape has willed all the personal property to her sisters and the children," exclaimed the widower, and with an indignant look he continued, "A law that permits such a state of things is a disgrace to the age. It belongs to the past, not the present. It's a disgrace to every lawmaker that such cruel, barbaric fossils are retained on the statute books of an enlightened people!"

J.—Is it any fault of the court, Mr. Crape? *We* are not law-makers. We are expounders. You must go to the Legislature for redress. This court, this beautiful Probate, is an executive branch of *political economy.* It is politic in all its ways with widowers."

Mr. C.—But, yer Honoress—

"There is no *but* in it," impatiently broke in the judgess, and the pink in her shell-like, lace-garnished ear turned crimson.

"It's a cruel thing," persisted Mr. Crape, as though he had not been interrupted, "for a parent to be deprived of the guardianship of minor children."

The judgess, with a cutting look and great severity, replied:

"Were you a suitable person, Mr. Crape, to have charge of your infants, your wife, a most estimable and upright woman, would never have deprived you of that privilege. She was the better judge and has acted wisely, undoubtedly; and I repeat the assertion, I shall respect her decision, and I believe I am supported, fully supported, by the intelligent and impartial juryesses."

"You are supported!" chimed in the many-voiced jury.

"Have you anything further to say, Mr. Crape?" continued the judgess, in the same severe tone.

"I have," replied Mr. Crape. "I look upon this

whole transaction as an outrage on human forbearance."

"Order! order!" shouted the clerkess, stamping the floor with her small, fashionably equipped foot. "You are out of order, sir," which so frightened Mr. Crape that he became quiet, and wept, and wept, and wept.

MR. CRAPE.

J.—I repeat the question: Have you anything further to say, widower? If you have, say it quickly, for this is your last opportunity. Too much time has been wasted upon your case already.

Mr. Crape turned his brimming eyes in the direction of his sisters-in-law, who were standing guard over their wards, and said beseechingly, 'I should like to kiss little Johnny good-bye."

J.—That is not permissible! It is wholly incompatible with court etiquette. The dignity and circumspection of beautiful Probate must not be trifled with in such an unprecedented manner.

"Little Johnny is my only son, and we are very

fond of each other," pleaded Mr. Crape, while the dew of fondness fell from his nose in crystal drops.

At this juncture little Johnny insisted on going to his father. His guardianesses had been able to keep him quiet until then, with copious supplies of sugar-plums and various mental visions of hobby-horses with real hair for manes and tails; but, when his mental and physical appetite was cloyed, his affectional nature asserted itself, and he craved for *father* when *mother* was under the sod.

"I 'onts my papa, I 'onts my papa! Let me do to my pa!" he shouted at the top of his small voice.

"Take that child out of court!" sternly commanded the judgess.

When the shrieks of his darling were lost in the distance, Mr. Crape sat down, and, losing all control over his feelings, groaned aloud.

J.—Mr. Crape, be a *man!* His guardianesses will do far better by little Johnny than you could possibly do. They will put him in a fashionable boarding-school for "*young gentlemen*," in the great, good, virtuous city, and he will sleep in a beautiful dormitory with a million other motherless cherubs, and be nourished with carbonic acid and other confections. Then, besides all these first-class advantages, he will be dressed in tights and taught the

German by Professor Fiddlesticks, which is far better for little Johnny's health and morals than his father's care and love could possibly be. At night he will kneel down beside his little, long coffin of an iron bedstead, with a white counterpane, like a shroud, over it, and say, "Now I lay me down to sleep, I pray the Lord my soul to keep. Yours truly, Johnny Crape."

"Among these beautiful, refining, intellectual surroundings little Johnny will forget the vulgar (natural affections) side of his nature; forget all about father and mother and the home of his childhood; forget how to laugh and cry. Little Johnny will be a little man then, which is a most wise and providential arrangement, and shows the perfection and wisdom of our learned women who make and enforce these beautiful laws; laws so humane, Christian and philanthropic; laws whose vigorous roots reach back to the dark ages, but whose branches are nourished by the sun and breath of civilization. The status of a nation's civilization is *measured* by its laws.

"We send our most accomplished and erudite women to the capitals of our states and nation. The stars pause in their course to listen to the wisdom which rises like incense to heaven, from the pure lips of these uncorruptible stateswomen. The air wafted through the pillared corridors and lofty arches of the storied fanes, consecrated to *Wisdom*, at these centres of ambition—is filled with myrrh and frankincense. The spotless legislatoressess go up to these temples, these law manufactories, these Meccas of petitions, to labor early and late for their constituents. They—the legislatoresses—never '*hop.*' The closing hours of these sessions are spent in dignified repose, for all bills and '*things*' have been carefully, prayerfully, timefully, prudently, passed upon. There is nothing left for them to do but to grasp hands in an amicable 'good-by!' and hasten to the bosoms of husbands and little ones."

During the judgess' long and beautiful speech, Mr. Crape had dried his red eyes with his ample handkerchief and got his feelings under control, and when she said, with a waive of her white hand (the one with the solitaire on the index finger), "You have nothing further to say, I trust, Mr. Crape," he quickly and spiritedly replied:

"*Certainly I have!*" and rising to his feet he adjusted his collar, edged with black, and continued: "Most wise, learned, and *just* judgess, when two people, and those two people are husband and wife, earn a fortune together and one of them dies, it seems to me that the survivor should succeed to the joint estate without administration."

"Hear, hear!" cried the clerkess; the seven learned counselloresses and the jury rose to their feet in a body, while three of the outside attorneyesses fainted dead away in the arms of the bystanders. The judgess, with a look of amazement on her handsome face, and a cold-steel glitter in her eyes, which pinioned Mr. Crape to the spot, where he stood like two stilettoes, exclaimed:

"What new-fangled heresy is this? Are the children not to be provided for? Are the wife's relations not to be provided for? Is this court, this beautiful Probate, not to be provided for? Is such wide-spread ruin and desolation, as such a step would involve, to be permitted? *Never*, widower, never! Why, man and mortal, do you know what you are talking about? Do you not know that *all* the property in the United States, real and personal, goes through this court every *thirty* years? That this beautiful institution could not live a day, nor an hour, nor a minute, nor a second, nor a *half* a second, were it not for the dismemberment of widowers' estates?"

As the judgess warmed in her subject she glowed like a beautiful furnace, and rising to her small feet, encased in French boots, she shook her jewelled hand, all doubled up, at the audacious widower, as she continued her eloquent denunciation in these never-to-be-forgotten words:

"Dare you stand there and insult the *Ermine* by promulgating the double-dyed heretical doctrine that *men* earn money in wedlock, and, per consequence, the home, with all its sacred associations, should not be broken up at the death of the wife and mother, and scattered to the four winds for the benefit of beautiful, composite, hungry Probate? This venerable and venerated custom is the perfection of a Christian civilization, the condensed extract of centuries. It must not, it *shall* not be polluted by unconsecrated hands."

As the judgess ceased speaking and resumed the "*revolver*," there was a burst of applause which shook beautiful Probate from turret to foundation-stone, and back again, but Mr. Crape remained standing, and, when the roar and tumult had subsided, said:

"I repeat, and emphasize the repetition, that the will of my wife robs me of all the property and of the guardianship of my minor children, which is a burning outrage. There is no blush deep enough to hide the shame of such an unnatural, diabolical law, that invites people to commit such crimes against the living, to take effect when they, the perpetrators, are dead. The creating of a guardian, for a child, other than its father, at the death of its mother, is against the laws of God and nature; and I pray, judgess, that you in your high position, will, in the name of justice, abrogate so much of the last will and testament of the late lamented Mrs. Crape as pertains to the care and protection of my babes."

J.—What, man! Would you presume to dictate to a mother, who has suffered for her children as no man can ever suffer, who shall or shall not be their guardian after her death?

Mr. C.—Am not *I* a parent as well as she? Don't I love my children? Haven't I provided a home for them? Am I of no importance in the world?

J.—I admit that you are—a necessary evil, a sort of vulgar fraction in the economy of life; a producer of wealth in its coarser fibre—*a money getter*. How does that compare, in the economy of life, with the finer and more subtle contributions of woman, the universal mother of the race? As dross to fine gold, as day to night, as an hour to eternity, as a grain of sand to the universe, as a drop of water to the seas that belt the earth. She is the producer of wealth in its *finer* fibre—life, and spirit, and the never-dying soul. These are her offerings, her contributions to the economy of life.

"Woman is the capstone of creation," continued the judgess with a radiant and triumphant look, "moulded and fashioned out of *live*, human material, whilst man, together with the other *lower* order of animals, was made out of the dull, lifeless clods of the valley. The spring cannot rise above its source! Be contented, widower, I can do nothing for you. *Your case is dismissed.*"

Mr. Crape and the hat with the bombazine band and flowing ends, and the black handkerchief with a white centre, moved slowly out of court, and faded from memory to all save his weeping and sorrowing babes. They, too, will forget him in time, or look upon him as a culprit who dared offend beautiful Probate, by asking to have control of their persons during minority.

A Contested Will

was the next case called. Eliakim Q. Snipe, the "relict" of Martha Jane Snipe, deceased, who in life was an apothecaryess, by profession, answered to the call, in person.

Eliakim Q. Snipe, was a long, lank, leathery visaged man, who sported a shock of well-brushed black hair, the sight of which would fill the breast of a saddler's apprentice with green and yellow envy, and his chin-whiskers would put to the blush the hairiest goat in the land. There was a wary, uncertain look in his (Eliakim Q. Snipe's) sharp eyes, that did not improve with acquaintance. His nose was a prominent feature, being remarkable for its length and irregularity. The smell end of it looked as though it had been blocked out, hewn to a point and abandoned—left in the rough, as it were, and the rough, unfinished part was as red as a beet—a perpetual indignant protest against the oversight of not being properly finished off.

There were no visible signs of *grief* about Mr. Snipe. He wore a soft-crowned hat with a dent in the side of it, tea-colored gloves, army-gray pantaloons, and a cutaway coat. He carried in his right hand a twisted cane, surmounted by a boar's head, and his whole appearance was peculiarly suggestive of an acorn-fed shoat after a hard winter.

Eliakim Q. Snipe looked about the court-room at the judgess, and at the seven learned counselloresses in an eager, but determined manner, and seemed to single out Miss Prudence Prim as a special eye-target. Miss Prim was a precise, cold-starched spinster, thin and tall, with a scant fleece of sandy hair twisted in a little knob on top of her head, from which dangled two starveling cork-screw curls. Her lips were thin, and her speaking voice was thin, but what it lacked in volume it made up in sharpness and penetration. She was a counselloress who always "*appeared*" for the court—for beautiful Probate, because she knew so much about marital relations, and the wants of widowers and motherless children, I suppose. She was a special Probate pleader, and a great favorite with counselloresses generally, for she sanctioned, or seconded rather, *all* "contingent fees."

Mr. Snipe scrutinized her so keenly that she twice dashed her hand before her face in order to break the offensive psycho-basilistic current. Not succeeding, she placed between herself and such imminent peril a little green hand-screen embossed with a white dove, holding in its mouth the olive branch of peace, emblematic of beautiful Probate. But on the reverse side of the little green hand-screen was embossed an alligator, swallowing a widower.

"Who is your counsel, Mr. Snipe?" questioned the judgess.

Mr. S.—"I have none, y'r Honoress. I intend to plead my own case."

J.—That is against the rulings of this court, Mr. Snipe. Were I to permit every widower to plead his own case, what would become of the practice of the *special* pleaders? beautiful Probate retainers, whose "appearance" in every and all cases affords them and their worthy families an honest support.

Mr. S.—This is why I wish to plead my own case, to save expense of counsel; Martha Jane must have been under mesmeric influence, when she made that will, which virtually leaves her poor widower out in the cold.

As Mr. Eliakim Q. Snipe finished the sentence, he shivered, and his teeth chattered as though an ague fit had overtaken him—and removing his tea-colored gloves, he buttoned the cutaway from top to bottom. This operation having been performed to the entire satisfaction of Mr. Snipe, he continued:

"I understand the *modus operandi* of this beautiful court. A few months ago my sister, Jane I. Depew, died, leaving, as it was supposed, a handsome fortune to her widower and children. But the estate has all melted away during the settlement. Young lawyeresses without number, who could not tell where their next meal, or the price of a night's lodging was to come from—sent in bills ranging all the way from fifty to five hundred dollars for "*ap-*

pearing" in the case, and these monstrous charges were allowed. Now, I am a legal heir to my late wife's estate, and propose to have a voice in its settlement, for which service I shall be paid five cents on a dollar.

J.—That is impossible, sir; you were not named in the will.

Mr. S.—Not *named* as an executor? Is the law so deficient that it does not recognize my *right* to succeed to the management of the estate, at the death of my wife, that was accumulated during marriage?

J. (*Aside*)—*What an absurd question!* Certainly not. What do men know about business matters? Mrs. Snipe has providentially appointed Jerusha Grit, and Tabathy Tite, both sound business women, to look after your best interest, and you have reason to congratulate yourself, Mr. Snipe, that you have fallen into such tender hands.

"Such a law is a travesty upon justice," exclaimed Mr. Snipe, getting red in the face, and, laying down his gloves and soft-crown, which up to this point had remained securely tucked under his arm, he continued with great warmth of manner to further unburden his mind on court practice, by saying:

"The law is not consistent, for it permits a wife

to will a small portion of the joint estate, gathered in wedlock, to her husband, in *all* the states, and in some of them it allows what is recognized as the 'widower's thirds;' and yet this consistent, cut-throat court denies a widower the careful supervision of such property as these humane provisions embrace. Does y'r Honoress call that consistency?"

"This court is not a debating school, Mr. Snipe," said the judgess, with a dark, portentous look, "and it has nothing to do with *consistency* whatever. I am on the bench to execute laws which are sanctioned by the combined wisdom of a great state—laws that had their birth among the aristocracy of primitive times. They are hoary with age, and, therefore, should be held in all sacredness, reverence, honor, high above the cavil of laymen and filibusters generally. The women who sanction these laws are known for their purity of character, their practical knowledge, their scientific attainments, their deep humility, their singleness of purpose. They have no bad habits; they never take bribes; they never impoverish the state's treasury by junketing parties; they never disappoint their constituents; they are never guilty of jobbery and corruption; they would scorn to put so much as their *little* finger in the till of the public treasury.

"To waive all further discussion on the subject, Mr. Snipe, I will say, once for all, that I shall adhere strictly to the text of the will," and with a sigh of relief the judgess was about to dismiss the case. But she had reckoned without her host, for Mr. Snipe again stood upon his feet (he had been refreshing himself by sitting down), and blandly requested that the will of the late Martha Jane Snipe be read in open court.

ELIAKIM Q. SNIPE.

Instantaneously Mr. Eliakim Q. Snipe became a magnet for every eye in court. But the persistent, pertinacious Eliakim sat down cool and unmoved, and, putting his hands in his pockets, listened with exasperating imperturbability to the last wishes of the dear departed.

LAST WILL AND TESTAMENT OF MARTHA JANE SNIPE.

Know all women by these presents, I, Martha Jane Snipe, being sound in mind and body, herein declare this instrument to be my last will and testament. After all lawful debts and charges against my estate are paid, I will, bequeath, and devise to my three children, Martha Jane, Matilda Ann, and Seth, two-thirds of all my property, real and personal, of which I die seized, share and share alike. To my beloved husband, Eliakim Q. Snipe, I will, bequeath, and devise the remaining third, to hold and to keep in *good repair* during his natural [not artificial] life, and at his death, I further provide that this portion of my said estate shall be divided among my three children in the same proportion as mentioned above. I appoint my dear friends and co-partners in business, Jerusha Grit and Tabathy Tite, guardians of my children, and executoresses of my estate, to serve without bonds, whereunto I have this day, in the year of our Lord, 1875, set my hand and seal. Amen!

MARTHA JANE SNIPE. (Seal.)

Witnesses, { SAMANTHA HART,
OTTIWELL WOOD.

CODICIL.

(*An after-thought.*)

In case any one of my three children should renounce faith in Close Communion, and go over to their father's creed, Episcopalian, I revoke so much of my will as regards the changeling's portion of my property, and cut the offender off with a two-bit piece. And I further provide, that in the event of such a dire calamity, that the culprit's portion shall be given, *at once*, to the First Close Communion Baptist Church, of which I am a member in good standing, to build a new immersion font. Should my beloved husband, Eliakim Q. Snipe, marry again, he, too, is to be cut off with a two-bit piece. The dead must not be forgotten with impunity, and their places filled with strangers.

After hearing the will and codicil read, Mr. Snipe rose up, and, rubbing his right ear till it glowed like a red-hot coal in a little nest of hair and whiskers, said: "I don't believe Marthy Jane ever made such a will as that. She was too sensible a woman. It's *agin natur* to live alone. The Bible commands us to multiply and replenish the earth, and how's a man to obey that command, I should like to know, without a wife?"

Mr. Snipe looked straight at counselloress Prudence Prim when he propounded this stunning question. She returned the look with eyes full of poniards, and starting to her feet, said, with cutting sarcasm:

"It is not necessary for the world's progress that *you* should ever duplicate yourself. When that command was given, men, by their vices, had not degenerated into—" Here Miss Prim's prudence came in, and she paused, an *awful* pause, and it remains a mystery to this day what animal the learned counselloress had in her mind's eye. But, judging from its expression, it must have been a terrible beast.

Mr. Snipe appeared far from resenting the thrust, for he sat right down, without another word, never taking his glistening eyes from the face of Miss Prim, and smiled, and smiled, while with tightly folded arms he held his breast in a close embrace.

"You seem to doubt the authenticity of this will, Mr. Snipe," said her Honoress, surveying the doubter with a look of unfeigned contempt and proud disdain.

"I do!" emphatically responded Mr. Eliakim Q. Snipe, tugging at his chin whiskers with a provoking grin.

J.—Are the witnesses in court, sir?"

Mr. S.—One of them—Mr. Wood—is present.

"Swear the gentleman," said the judgess, peremptorily.

When the witness was called to the "chair," there was a perceptible titter among the bystanders, and the seven learned counselloresses, having no feathers on their steel pens to chew, nearly gnawed the ends of their seven thumbs off, in order to keep their seven learned faces straight.

The cause of this undignified commotion in beautiful Probate was the remarkable appearance of the witness, Mr. Wood. He looked like an overgrown bisected carrot in breeches and necktie. He was pumpkin color, and freckled, and cross-eyed, and hare-lipped, and, if mother Nature ever had anything to do with him, she must have been on a lark at the time, "for he was a sight to shake the midriff of despair with laughter." The end of his nose and the tips of his ears (which swept the ceiling) worked and wiggled, whenever he spoke, like a dog's. Both his eye-teeth were gone, or uncut, and through the levees of his mouth, caused by their absence, the tobacco-juice trickled in a steady stream down the valleys of his chin. His feet were gotten up regardless of leather, and taking him as a whole he was as "*quare a craythur*" as one would encounter in a lifetime.

"What is your name?" said the clerkess, perking up her mouth, and adjusting her spectacles, preparatory to swearing him.

"*Ottiwell Wood!*" bawled the curious specimen, holding up his hand and kissing the "caff" instead of the "book."

"How do you *spell* it?" asked the somewhat puzzled judgess. To which Mr. Wood replied, in the same stentorian key,

"O double T, I double U, E double L, double U, double O D."

At this a *double* titter ran around the room, and the seven rosy mouths of the seven learned counselloresses were hidden in white cambric. The judgess's face put on an amused and undignified expression as she surveyed the witness through her quizzing glass. Having satisfied her curiosity, she laid aside the glass, and, resuming her accustomed serenity and lofty demeanor, said: " Were you present, Mr. Wood, at the signing of this will?"

WITNESS.—Sartain I wuz, zur—y'r Honor, I means.

J.—Do you think Mrs. Snipe was *compos mentis* when she signed this will, Mr. Wood? Remember, sir, you are upon oath. Don't *perjure* yourself.

" Perfectly *cumpus*, zur, an' she sartainly *ment ter* dew it," replied Mr. Wood, not at all disconcerted by the judgess's admonition, while his mulberry eyes played cross-cuts with the laughter-convulsed jury.

J.—Did you ever hear her speak on religious subjects, Mr. Wood?

W.—Yis, zur, I did. She wuz a hard-shell Baptist, she wuz; b'l'ev'd in 'mershun—duckin' clean *under*, ye know—ah' she b'l'ev'd in 'lection an' pre-ord'rnashun. She wuz set like a vise on *pre*-ord'nashun. B'l'ev'd in brimstun, an' sich.

J.—Did you ever hear her mention the Episcopalians?

W.—You *bet* yer butes I did, orfen. She couldn't bear the hyfalutin 'piscopalians—said they wuz bound ter toast fur want o' water.

J.—Do you think, Mr. Wood, that she would disinherit a child for embracing their doctrines?

W.—She'd dew it certain, fur she didn't b'l'eve anything 'ud take out sin but water.

"That is sufficient, sir," said the judgess, with an impatient wave of her jeweled hand; and the witness, to the intense relief of the seven learned counselloresses, descended from the chair. The clerkess removed from her head a copy of the *Evening Post*, under which she had taken shelter at the first shower of tobacco-juice, which flew in all directions every time Mr. Wood spoke. Her desk was just below and nearly in front of the witness-chair, which placed her in full range of the saliva, and, fully realizing her perilous position, she had resorted to paper breastworks in order to protect her back-hair from contamination. But the "cover" was damaging to the beauty of the clerical lady, for it gave her the remarkable appearance of a ferret in goggles peering from under a hedge.

"I should like to have this *just* court explain," said Eliakim Q. Snipe, again standing up, and rubbing his right ear until every hair in the shock above it stood on end, "how it reconciles justice with fraud!"

J.—*Fraud!* Do you understand the definition of that word, Mr. Snipe?

Mr. S.—I think I do, y'r Honoress. It is to

forcibly take away from a man what is his by right. I have a right to my children, as the author of their being—at their mother's death. I have a right to the property that my wife and I have conjointly earned—at her death; and I have a right to the undisturbed possession of the family mansion—at her death. I look upon this court, this *beautiful* Probate, as but little removed from a *prize* tribunal, when it robs me of these natural rights.

This outburst brought Miss Prim to her feet again. Laying the right forefinger in the palm of her left hand, she made a step forward, and, looking full in the face of the unabashed widower, asked, in vibrant falsetto:

"Eliakim Q. Snipe, do you come here to malign this court in its open face? Do you expect to stigmatize it with impunity, simply because it protects your motherless children from the terrors of a stepmother? because it protects the property, which she left for their support, from being squandered by her widower? Do you expect to do this unscourged, sir? If you do, sir, you are mistaken, sir, for not one hair of the 'Ermine' shall be carelessly, causelessly, ruthlessly, and heinously ruffled, without swift retribution, sir. This you have sought to do, sir, without cause or provocation, sir, and for such barefaced effrontery and malice aforethought, you shall be made an example of, as a warning to all audacious offenders. You, sir, are guilty of *contempt* of *court*, and shall be 'sent *up*' for a million days." At which the jury clapped their hands, and the seven learned counselloresses exchanged looks of unqualified approval.

"I confirm and applaud the learned counselloress's decision," exclaimed the judgess, "and declare that for contempt of court and unprecedented temerity, Eliakim Q. Snipe, relict of the late lamented Martha Jane Snipe, be sent up for the term of a million days. *The court is dismissed.*"

Amidst the rustle of paper, the clash of blue bags, and ripples of merry laughter, the triumphant court broke up, and the sheriffess, Dorothy Grip, led forth the now thoroughly subdued prisoner, Eliakim Q. Snipe, like a lamb to the slaughter.

SCENE THE ELEVENTH.

CLOSING REMARKS.

Finis coronat opus.

THERE must be a dessert to a feast—a feast of chaff, even—whipped cream, floating islands, or *soufflé*, something feathery to top off the substance. Perhaps you, my dear readers, may argue that there is no substance to chaff, and therefore no top to "*off*," no bottom, no middle, no circumference, no height, no depth, no anything.

Well, if you do, we shan't quarrel about it, for I promised you as much, no more, in the beginning. You, some of you, rebelled against *Probate Confiscation* (wheat), said it was too much for you; said that it was indigestible, made you dyspeptic; said that your whole physical and mental well-being cried aloud for an antidote, an anti-dyspeptic composition, and I, being of a humane disposition and of an obliging turn of mind, have given you "Chaff," which is a sovereign remedy for dumps, dyspepsia, melancholia, and low spirits of every complexion. Taken in large quantities, it is as digestible as bran, and quite as nutritious. It can be indulged in *ad libitum*. There is no danger from an overdose.

You may feel that you have had an overdose already. But have I not kept my word? Does not the end support the beginning? Have I not piped for you to dance with joy and thanksgiving? Have I not caused you to rejoice and be exceeding glad that there is such a blessed providential institution as beautiful Probate? After perusing these pages, does not every loving husband and father want to die, in order that his dear wife and babes may enjoy the fostering care of beautiful Probate? Does not every gentle and tender wife and mother long to be widowed, so that she may be enfolded in the fond and all-absorbing arms of beautiful Probate? Does not every sensible minor child pray to be orphaned, so that *it* may be fondled in the ample lap and nourishing bosom of beautiful Probate? None but those who are wilfully blind can, after looking at the pen-sketch which I have drawn, fail to see the excellences, the humanities, the transcendent loveliness of this *beautiful Probate*.

"Oh, long may it wave,
O'er the land of the free, and the home of the brave!"

"But what of the *dramatis personæ?*" you pertinently ask. "Are we not to have a parting glance at their faces?" "*Certainly*," I make reply. "The picture would be incomplete without this last finishing touch. You shall be treated to a biographical sketch, a sort of running portrait or dissolving view of each one of *importance*, that has figured in this modern drama. You shall know something of his or her present condition and past disposition."

THE SEVEN KITS

were disposed of in this wise. I trust you, my dear readers, will not think so illy of me as to imagine for one moment that when I left the "Dovery" I left my pets to shirk for themselves. Ah! no; I am too true a friend for such a heartless deed.

One morning, soon after the departure of Delilah (the Dovery never seemed like a Dovery after she and Nellie were gone), when I was casting about in my mind how to dispose of my "good omens," Mr. Wing Wang, my laundryman, came up the steps and saw, for the first time, the seven beauties in a mottled group, sunning themselves on the piazza.

"Blessee me hartee! Miss Toe," he exclaimed, greedily eyeing the happy heap, "wat plenty katee you gotee."

"Yes," I replied. "Do you know of any one who wants a cat, Mr. Wing Wang?"

"O yisee, plentee. Me wantee katee; my cousin, he wantee katee. I putee he in my bagee;" and suiting the action to the word, and before I took in the situation, he laid hold of Bigeye, and thrust him headforemost into a straw-matting bag which he carried under his arm. A cat-abductor undoubtedly. Poor Bigeye was not "*kat*"-napped without a struggle. He yowled lustily, and left a running mark on the hand of his tormentor. Mr. Wing Wang's eyes gleamed with satisfaction as he remarked,

"He plentee fatee, Miss Toe, *plentee* fatee." Then too late I remembered that *fat* kittens and *fat* puppy-dogs go to pot in the Flowery Kingdom, and hinted as much to the man of the tub, but his reply was,

"Oh, me lovee he katee, me lovee he. He belly goodee. He *fatee*."

"I'm afraid, Mr. Wing Wang, you 'lovee he' at the end of chopsticks," I replied, stroking Bobbins's back. I had caught her up as she was flying past me, in great fright, when Bigeye was bagged. There was not another cat to be seen. Cats, as a rule, don't love Chinamen half as well as Chinamen love cats.

I could not endure the thought of Bigeye's lonely condition down among the smells of Chinatown, and said so to Mr. Wing Wang. He was eager to have Bobbins, too, and promised that they should have "plentee milkee an' metee, 'nough to makee him lun fastee after the lat. Latee plentee in my house. One katee not hap 'nough to killee the lat." When he had finished his statement, of the case, and Bobbins had joined Bigeye in the bag, he swung it over his shoulder, and went his way rejoicing.

Poor dear kits! I could hear them crying, and protesting, and reproaching me all the way down the long flight of stairs that led up to the Dovery, and in a few moments Sally came to me with such an injured and indignant look on her motherly face, as she inquired where her darlings were, that I was half inclined to raise the cry of "*stop thief*," and thus recover our treasures. That night I had horrible dreams of fricasseed kittens and stewed rats.

The next two—I parted with them in pairs, so that they could hunt in couples, and not pine alone—I gave to sister Gertie as a Christmas gift. They were my special favorites—Rutherford B. and Samuel J. Rutherford B. we called *Bepo* for short, and he was shortly after stolen from my sister; and Sam. Tilden had kittens. A clear case of "mistaken identity."

Sally I left in charge of the Dovery. She being a splendid mouser and moler, and, not having had the mole-ranch auctioned off yet, I felt perfectly contented to leave her and the fifth kitten on the terrace, to cater for themselves.

Bismarck was never seen after the serenade, and, as his white favor and a piece of fur were found the next morning on the Sacramento pier, we surmised that he was in league or love with some salt-water owless, and that with her he had returned to his old home in Alaska. Between you and I, dear readers, I believe the owless was the *wooer*, and in order to convince you that I am supported, and not alone in this belief, I will quote the following lines from "*As You Like It:*"

> " Oh, the owl and the pussy-cat went to sea
> In a beautiful pea-green boat.
> Said the owl to the pussy-cat, 'Pussy, my love,
> What a beautiful pussy you be,
> What a *beautiful* pussy you be, you be,
> What a beautiful pussy you—*be!*' "

DELILAH HAWTHORN HERRING

still lives in her cottage embowered home in Sacramento. Husband, home and friends have acted like a tonic on the sharp features of our friend, rounding them into comeliness, and matronly beauty. Mr. Herring looks ten years younger than he did on the memorable night of the wedding. He declares that he will stake his "bottom dollar," that no "feller" ever made so much out of a visit as he did during that never-to-be-forgotten week in the Cave or Dovery, he don't care a picayune which name is used, so long as he played "dove and Delilah caved in."

I shall not dare *visit* them again, for he says that he has got a Mr. *Sardine* picked out for me, and that it is "neck or nothing," and he is determined it shall be *neck*, and that I shall marry Sardine whether *Barkis* is willin' or not. Now as I know something about the power of *will*, I, with all my boastful courage, dare not go to Sacramento again, for this reason: I can't abide anything done up in oil.

JACK

has removed from Los Angeles to Oakland, taking Esculapius and family with him for medicinal and culinary purposes. Although in the ripeness of doghood, he has not forgotten the home of his youth —nor the friends of bygone days.

TRUESPUNK KILLKINS,

singular to relate, is still single. Since we last saw him he has lost a molar, and the plain on top of his head has become more extended. The pink note paper with the skipping cupids remains untouched, for the period of sentiment has passed with Mr. Killkins. It ended with his last abortive effort at love-making. Without the aid of some determined widow he is sure to die a bachelor.

THISTLE,

Spiderwort and Tangleweed are all in capital health and spirits. Prosperity and abundance are constant guests at their firesides, for their numerous fields (widows' fields) are whitest during hard times. Bi Barnacle is laid up with the gout, whilst Snifter has resorted to a sea of flannel, to ease his rheumatism. Old O'Flaherty and Toombs are in their normal condition—unceasingly laboring for the sole benefit of the widow and the fatherless(?) and the cashier's ditto. The mediumistic, earnest, and anxious go-betweens are still in the middle of money speculations and loan negotiations. Let them alone.

THE CHAMBER OF COMMERCE

is like a vigorous tree laden with unblemished fruit, for the members have so far recovered, that they have discontinued ice-baskets and slings (for their arms). The carriers' feet have grown out, and the insane paper-dealers are healed of their malady, and have returned, from Stockton, to the bosoms of their families. The steam paddies have gone back to the hills, and the dredgers to Mission Creek, leaving the waters of the bay in placid repose.

CHARLES DE YOUNG

is still happy, handsome, and prosperous, although the trillion-million-billion libel suit hangs over his head like a black nimbus, or the sword of Ulysses. He continues a bachelor in spite of Cupid's darts, with which, as I have said before, he bristles like St. Sebastian, or a prickly pear, or a thorn hedge. Not one of these murderous arrows have as yet proved deadly enough to reach his heart. The *Chronicle's* circulation has increased a million-fold since its immersion in the bay. It has doubled its two-legged and quadrupled its four-legged force. This is owing to the popularity of its salt-water contributors. It now numbers on its editoral staff, sharks, eels, seals, and other intellectual fry, and it expects to employ *pickerel* as soon as that gamy fish is captured.

MY WHITE ERMINE

still occupies beautiful Probate's *revolver*, and still metes out justice in a *still* way to widows and orphans. His perquisites do not count up $20,000 a year, ah, no! no, no, no! *My* Ermine is satisfied with his modest $5,000. He it is who adjusts all legacies and settlements, and always

> "Holds the balance of success (for beautiful Probate)
> With much precision and address."

As regards *settlements*, he has proved himself a match for Sir John Pratt, who, every one knows, was a model of equity. To remove all doubts on the subject of sound and discriminating ability on the part of this learned majesterial functionary, I will quote *one* of his decisions, feeling sure that with all fair minded people one will suffice:

> " A woman having a settlement,
>   Marries a man with none;
> The ' *Question* ' was, he being dead,
>   ' If that she had was gone? '
> Quoth Sir John Pratt—' Her settlement
>   *Suspended* did remain
> *Living* the husband: But him *dead*,
>   It doth *revive* again!'"

All my Ermine's ways are ways of pleasantness, and all my Ermine's paths are paths of peace. His tender, capacious heart is still the habitation of all widows' woes, for he remains a widower in order to be ever ready with the door of this palpitating habitation wide open to receive, as guests, all new-comers —I mean by this all new woe-comers. Perhaps I should say, right here, that it is only the self-abnegating, clinging-vine sort of widow that gets taken into this heart of hearts. The "*stiff necks*" sit on the steps outside, and I don't believe they want to get in. I didn't. I belong to the outsiders.

MR. PUMPUM

is still pleading, pleading, and cross-examining witnesses. He is longer, to all appearances, gaunter and more eager to trip up the timid and unwary than ever, and he is more repulsive looking than ever. His nose has been swaddled up in the red bandanna, and played upon so often that it has permanently taken on the intense rubicund of the *mouchoir*, to the unqualified disgust of its owner—nose owner. It seems to throw down its gauntlet, as a challenge, for a tweak every time Mr. Pumpum looks in the glass. On these not infrequent occasions, he feels as though he would have the obnoxious and insulting member extricated or amputated, or blown off with gunpowder, and a proper, well mannered nose of a becoming tint manufactured out of wax take its place. But a second thought—Mr. P. is pestered with second thoughts at such times—convinces him that the first tuneful blast sent whistling through the well complexioned wax substitute would annihilate it, blow it to atoms, and thus leave the front side of his head a vast *plain* instead of a mountainous region.

Mr. Pumpum's pleadings have made him "*well-to-do*" in this world's goods. He lives in a sumptuous redwood front with seven gables; keeps seven servants, and has a farm of seven acres, stocked with seven cows, in the country. He is the *lawful* father of seven sons and seven handsome daughters. His seven sons he is training for the bar, and his seven handsome daughters he is training for wives. The seven sons take after the father in personal appearance, and the seven handsome daughters take after the mother in personal appearance.

THE CLERK

looks like a little bundle of old parchment. Time has a withering, warping effect on him. He is obliged to wear loaded soles to his shoes to prevent his being blown away—like a Katydid. Gravitation has no more effect on him than it has on thistledown. But whatever loss he may have sustained in avoirdupois, is more than counterbalanced in augmented pomp. He is like a soap-bubble—all swell. Don't touch him for fear of a collapse.

The scribe is in his old place in the corner, scribbling down *important* testimony. The bystanders, and the special Probate pleaders, and the spittoons, are all in their appropriate places—beautiful Probate.

Mrs. O'Mulligan still keeps lodgers on Clover Street, but takes none but *single* gentlemen. Beauty Honeysuckle is married to a Mr. Brier. The Dovery has gone back to first principles, and is occupied by a captain and his (supposed to be) wife. Messrs. Wimple and Dumpty are in slippers and dressing-gowns; the former smiling and twirling his thumbs, the latter dozing over his *Evening Post*.

San Francisco has got a new constitution and expects to rival Methuselah in years. It is a beautiful constitution—almost as handsome as beautiful Probate. California's wisest, handsomest, and most accomplished sons manufactured it to *order*.

BEAUTIFUL PROBATE

in the State of New York. "But why do you speak of New York laws?" exclaim my dear readers. Quite right! Knowledge is the beginning of wisdom. I will tell you why, I am a daughter of the Empire State, and consequently know all about her beautiful laws of succession, inheritance, etc. I am very proud of my native State, proud of my native state's beautiful Probate system, proud of my native state's noble sons, my dear brothers, who make and enact these beautiful laws for the benefit of the widows and orphans of the Empire State. I am so proud of my brothers and the bountiful provisions of beautiful Probate, that I could not stay my pen if I would, from making an undying chronicle of the facts, and thus shower forth the light of their acts on the evil and the good, on the just and on the unjust. This I am determined to do. I am conscientiously consistent and pertinaciously persistent. You will find consistency running like a thread on fire through all these luminous pages.

Excelsior is the motto of my own beloved state, and excelsior is the watchword of all my beloved brethren in the State Legislature. No other state has excelsior for its motto, therefore the laws and the lawmakers of my own dear state are immeasurably above all the other states and lawmakers, with the exception of Delaware. The laws affecting the rights of women are magnificent in Delaware. What she lacks in length and breadth of territory, she makes up in height and depth of wisdom—in her lawmaking. The provisions made for the widow and the fatherless, as against the will of the husband and father, are *sublime* in Delaware. I am obliged to take off my "*bunit*" every time I think of them.

No Delawarian widow's life is harassed and tormented out of her with the care of *personal* property, if the will of her defunct lord and master relieves her of such perplexing and bewildering cares. No widow-mother is compelled by the humane laws of Delaware to have the care and annoyances of her offspring. What a *relief* to mothers!

The mothers and widows of the Empire State have the same safeguards thrown around them as the Delawarian mothers and widows have. These are the only *Northern* States where widows can be relieved (by wills) of *all* personal property—which in the present days of commerce is so much larger than real. These states cease to be exclusive, however, when it comes to the question of the guardianship of minor children; for Rhode Island and many other states in the fair sisterhood, north of Mason and Dixon's line, are humane and Christian enough to relieve wives and mothers, by the wills of tender, loving, thoughtful, careful husbands and fathers—living or dead—of the trouble of their own babes.

In the year of our Lord 1874, my astute brethren in the Legislature wiped out of the Revised Statutes of New York every vestige of an error in regard to the rights of widows and orphans, and the law as it stands to-day (1879), in the Empire State, challenges the admiration of christendom, for there have been no changes whatever, as regards the rights of widows, since 1874. Right! A *perfect* law should not be changed.

You, my dear readers, are eager to know just what these perfect laws are; I, my dear readers, am eager to have you know just what these perfect laws are. There should be no secrets between us. *Friends* never have secrets. I hope we *are* friends, I feel amicably toward you, and trust the feeling is reciprocal.

You will be surprised at the marvelous wisdom and far-sightedness of my brothers. Solomon's wisdom compared with theirs shows as a glow-worm beside the sun. I will show you how kind they are —they are full of mother's milk. I will show you how tender-hearted they are—more tender than an unshelled chicken. I will show you how brave they are—more brave than Pompey's lion. But why enumerate their various and varied excellences? The laws which they have made, or sanctioned, proclaim their praises trumpet-tongued. Here they are garnished or embellished with a few running comments by your author.

As all widows and orphans wear "*homespun*," the law, made by my dear brothers, provides, proclaims, and declares that "all *spinning wheels and weaving looms* shall be exempt from seizure by creditors," or the husband's kindred. Any one must have eyes of stone not to see the colossal wisdom of such a provision. Also "all *sewing machines* and *knitting machines*." Here, again, one is lost in speechless admiration. For what is the good of web-homespun without a sewing machine? Does it not have to be cut out and sewed up and down and across, around the corners and through the middle, and down the centre?

"Seam and gusset and band, band and gusset and seam."

And then what wisdom and warmth crops out of knitting machines, in the likeness or form of socks, and stockings, and mittens, and comforters, and wristlets, and undergear, and garters, and nightcaps.

"But where," you ask, "is the *wool* to come from

that is to be knitted on 'knitting machines,' spun on 'spinning wheels,' and woven on 'weaving looms'? Where?" The law guards against such an emergency, for law detests an emergency as much as nature detests a vacuum, by furnishing every widow with ten sheep. If she don't own sheep the humane and obliging legislature manufactures them to order, and the wool which is to be "spun, knitted, and woven" is from the backs of these ten sheep. The legislature further provide that these ten sheep shall have food for "*sixty days*" before they are turned into "chops and tomato sauce." The widow and her children have food and housing provided them by the same thoughtful humanitarians for a like period of time—then comes Lent.

There are other ample and munificent provisions, made by my dear brothers the legislators, such as "*one table.*" The social position of the table is not defined. This omission is somewhat perplexing. It might cause strife betwixt the widow and executors and the husband's kindred. No one knows whether it is to adorn drawing-room, dining-room, bed-room, work-room, wash-room, store-room, hall or kitchen.

"*Six chairs*" are also bountifully and providentially provided to sit on at the *one* table. This limits the number of orphans to five—which is wise.

Large families are not to be encouraged these hard times. They eat too much. Five hungry orphans and one hungry widow are quite enough for beautiful Probate to feed for sixty days. That is what the legislators think, that is what beautiful Probate thinks, that is what the upright executors think, that is what the husband's relatives think, that is what I think, and I have no doubt but that my thinking readers will think the same.

We are left in doubt and conjecture, my dear readers, as regards the kind or sort of chairs our brothers had in their mind's eye when they set down the generous half dozen. I am puzzled to know if they are spring-bottom, windsor, cane, stuffed, armed and castered, or camps. I would advise *camps*, for then when widows and orphans desire to change their base and occupy another room, or sit at dinner, or go to bed, they can fold their chairs, like the tents of the Arabs, and as quietly steal into dining-room, bed-room, or parlor, as the Bedouin of the desert steals a march on the unwary traveller.

"*Six plates*" are also mercifully provided, one for each chair. Here again is wisdom personified by *limitation*. A small number of plates, as compared with a large number, saves time, and croton, and soap, and the wear and tear of dishcloths. Cabbage, potatoes, and parsnips are to be served hot in the pot, or skillet, or frying-pan, for there are no platters mentioned.

"*Twelve knives and forks.*" Too many by *half*. No reasonable widow wants more knives than plates and chairs. "*Twelve tea-cups and saucers*" are set down, but no tumblers. Another error, for it encourages orphans to indulge in the intoxicating beverage of the *cup* instead of sparkling water. "*One sugar-pot, one milk-pot, one tea-pot,*" but no hot-water pot. The wisdom of my brothers again admits of a doubt. For what is a tea-pot without its concomitant, a hot-water pot? It is cruel to divorce these sociable pots, besides it tends to strong tea. A double waste—it diminishes the tea and unstrings the nerves. Widows' nerves should be kept well strung on a taut string.

"*Twelve spoons.*" Have you observed, my dear readers, how all the various and sundry household utensils and things run through our dear brothers' heads in dozens and half dozens, like their shirts, and stockings, and pocket-handkerchiefs, and collars, and cuffs? Habit holds them in so tight a grasp that the ludicrous crops out of their arithmetical calculations in spite of their profound wisdom. In counting out the spoons they forget to designate whether the said spoons are to be tea, table, or dessert; whether they are to be of wood, iron, pewter, brass, silver, or plated. This is two spoons to every mouth. Quite unnecessary, my brethren, quite. I make one silver-plated teaspoon answer every purpose in life, and I am a widow and a half-orphan.

Added to these munificent provisions, the noble sons of the Excelsior State allow a widow to keep her Bible and fifty school-books, and other nameless household stuff, providing always that she has it, to the value of $150. Grand! isn't it?

"Go ring the bells and fire the guns."

But what's this? I've left out the *pigs—dear me*, worse and worse, I've left out the *cow*. The widow is to have two pigs and one cow—no, one cow and two pigs. My dear brothers call the two pigs *swine*. They say "*two cows and one swine, and the pork of such swine.*" This must be a pleasantry on the part of my dear brethren, or else the law of New York resembles the law of Pennsylvania on this point. There a widow has no legal right to the body of her husband after the breath is out of it; here, judging from the mooted provision, a widow has no legal right to the carcass of her swine after the breath is out of it. Ownership, in each case, consists in breath. At its expiration the title expires. Curious, isn't it? This calls for an investigating committee.

Fearing that I may have left out some of the *generous provisions*, for the widow and the fatherless, and in order to doubly impress upon your minds every point of beauty, every vantage ground of excellence, I have gathered them—the generous provisions—all up in one charming bundle of jingle, and give them to you, my dear readers, *in nuce*. Shake it, and you will hear the music.

THE WIDOW'S PORTION.

" *All spinning-wheels* " to spin the thread,
" *All weaving-looms* " to weave the web;
" *Fifty school-books*," do you see?
" *One Bible* " keeps them company.
" *One machine* " for to knit the shirts,
" *One machine* " for to sew the skirts;
" *Stoves*," how many it does not say,
" *Family pictures*," too, may stay.
" *Ten sheep, their fleeces, yarn, and cloth*,"
" *One cow, two swine, and pork thereof*,"
With hay, and grass, and corn, and swill,
For " *sixty days* " they'll have their fill.
Beneath her roof-tree " *sixty days* "
The widow clasps her babe and prays.
Then law-clad guardians loose the clasp
And baby drops from mother's grasp.

"*Beds and bedding, and bedsteads*" (see !
What generous fellows my brothers be).
With "*proper apparel*" for every one,
Widow and daughter, widow and son.
"*One table,*" just one, *one*, ah! *one*,
"*Six chairs,*" a princely gift! Well done!
"*Twelve knives and forks,*" a *double* six,
"*Six plates,*" no *double* in *this* six,
"*Twelve*" saucy "*saucers*" holding "*cups*"
With tea and sugar, take a sup.
"*One sugar-dish, one milk-pot,*" bold,
"*One tea-pot and twelve spoons,*" all told,
Add to this munificent store
"*One hundred and fifty dollars*" more
Of household stuff—not named above—
And *fathomed is* my brothers' love.

After this careful, *double* enumeration of the bounties and blessings of beautiful Probate (If any one doubts the accuracy of these statements, let him turn to the appendix.), are you, my dear readers, surprised that I am in love with my own State and statesmen? Cold must be the heart that fails to beat with accelerated emotion at the revelation of such magnanimity! Dull must be the comprehension not to see the full-blown blossom of *chivalry* in "*six chairs;*" the tender chord of sympathy and good fellowship in "*one teapot;*" the milk of human kindness overflowing in "*one milk-pot;*" the perfection of "*gallantry* and *protection*" displayed in the "*sheep*" reservation; the lavish bounty of "*twelve spoons*," which gives every widow and orphan the luxury of eating mutton-broth with both hands; the royal bestowal of "*spinning-wheels and weaving looms*," of "*knitting-machines* and *sewing-machines*," which encourages industry, the palladium of a nation's prosperity; the colossal grandeur of "*one table;*" the dazzling splendor of "*six plates;*" the penetrating wisdom and incisive forethought which coruscates on the "*twelve knives*," and their companions, the "*forks.*" Magnificent!

Now comes the parting. Dear readers, I'm in tears; how are you? But keep up heart; we shall meet again in the "*Battle of the Book*," the book of books. I have visited so many charming places, states, cities, country towns, and villages, in my probate pilgrimage up and down the land and across the continent, that I must speak of them in all praise; and I must also speak in all praise of the charming people whom I have met in the different towns, cities, villages, and country-seats where I have been so often and hospitably entertained. Therefore, I shall, at my earliest convenience, show you the faces of these hospitable entertainers at the point of the pen, together with a kaleidoscopic view of the topographical peculiarities of each of the localities visited, for they have much to do with the character and eccentricities of the people.

The *"Battle of the Book"* will be the last of the charming series on the beautiful subject of Probate Courts. It will be the sequel to its fellows, P. C. and P. C. A modern *Pilgrim's Progress*, rivalling the adventures of *Robinson Crusoe*, or the *Innocents Abroad*. By the time it appears, you will be anxious to hear from me again, and I shall be anxious to have you, for we have jogged along together over the rough places so pleasantly thus far, that we shall meet in the *Battle of the Book* as old friends— veterans in war, and promulgators of peace: but for the time being we part in peace.

I desire that this parting may be solemn, dignified, and impressive; therefore, I propose that our last moments together be emblematic of the expiring swan—that the sweet bud of sympathy may blossom in symphony; a melodious "*good-by*" that will linger in our memories like the perfume of fresh flowers. Let us rise and sing an " *Ode* " to beautiful Probate. Could there be anything more appropriate? At the close of the song the curtain will be rung down and the candles blown out. Let us sing. All join in the chorus.

ODE TO BEAUTIFUL PROBATE.

Beautiful Probate! Lovely! Sweet!
  With lilies in your hair,
And pity in your tender eyes,
  Your hands are pure and fair.

Chorus.

    Beautiful, beautiful Probate,
    Joyfully, joyfully sing,
    Beautiful, beautiful Probate,
    Joyfully, joyfully sing.
      Pro—o—bate!

Rejoice, rejoice, and gaily sing!
  Widows and orphans, sing!
You'll be housed and fed *sixty* days,
  Without one ring, ding, ding.

Sing, *weaving looms* and *spinning-wheels*,
  And *knitting* for a medal.
Sing, *cow* and *swine*, and *pork thereof*,
  While *sewing* with a treadle.

Sing, *fifty dollars* household stuff,
  And plus it with a "*hunner*."
Sing, *six* in chairs, and *twelve* in spoons,
  One table. That's a stunner!

Sing, teapot *one*, and *milk-pot*, too,
  And count your *cups*, a dozen;
Six plates, *one* sugar-pot, and stoves,
  And keep your *wheel* a-buz'n.

Sing, beds and bedding, knives and forks,
　And petticoats and pictures,
The widow's "*proper orniments*,"
　And other household fixtures.

Then bend the knee and bare the brow,
　And swing the censer high.
Make hill and dale with echoes ring
　Up to the vaulted sky.

CHORUS.

Beautiful, beautiful Probate,
　Joyfully, joyfully sing!
Beautiful, beautiful Probate,
　Joyfully, joyfully sing!
　　Pro—o—bate!

APPENDIX.

THE STOW BILL,

ENTITLED

"An Act for the Protection of Widows."

SECTION 1. When a man dies leaving a last will and testament wherein he has appointed executors to the exclusion of his widow, then, in all such cases, the surrogate of the county, wherein said will shall be probated, shall, on application of the widow of the deceased, grant and issue letters testamentary, to said widow, if she is legally competent and not otherwise objectionable, in the same manner as though she had been named in the will, she to be vested with the same powers and bound by the same obligations under said will as they are, and such widow shall have the sole guardianship of the persons of her minor children, she being in every respect qualified and approved by the proper court having jurisdiction.

SECTION 2. After the payment of all debts, and the proper charges against the estate, one-third of the *personal* property left by a deceased husband, shall, in all cases, belong to his widow absolutely.

PETITION IN SUPPORT OF THE BILL.

To the Honorable Senate and Assembly:

The petition of the undersigned citizens of the State of New York, respectfully represents: That a widow is entitled to a proportionately large share of the property left by her deceased husband, and that where men are appointed, to her exclusion, executors of his last will and testament, she often experiences serious inconveniences from delay and expense in obtaining what the law allows her. Therefore, your petitioners pray, that as a simple act of justice, you will enact that no last will and testament made by a deceased husband shall bar the right of his widow, when she is legally competent and not otherwise objectionable, from having an active voice in the settlement of the estate; that she, upon application to the surrogate of the county wherein the last will and testament of her deceased husband is probated, may have letters testamentary granted and issued to her, if she is legally competent and not otherwise objectionable, in the same manner as the executors named therein, and that in every respect she be vested with the same powers and bound by the same obligations as they are; and that such widow shall have the sole guardianship of the persons of her minor children, she being in every respect qualified and approved by the court having proper jurisdiction. And your petitioners further pray that after the payment of all debts and proper charges against the estate, one-third of all the *personal* property left by a deceased husband shall, in all cases, belong to his widow absolutely.

GEORGE WILLIAM CURTIS,
HENRY W. BELLOWS,
J. S. SHULTZ,
HENRY BERGH,
A. V. STOUT,
WM. A. HALL,
PETER COOPER,
O. B. FROTHINGHAM,
JAMES W. SIMONTON,
OSWALD OTTENDORFER,
B. F. TRACY,
A. A. REDFIELD,
T. W. HOLCOMB,
M. V. MCDANIEL,
A. P. VAN GIESEN,
S. L. CALDWELL,
J. BACKUS,
CYRUS MACY,
DANIEL W. GUERNSEY,
C. SWAN,
JAMES MAKIN,
JOHN F. SMYTH,
HENRY L. LAMB,
JAMES MCWADE,
A. VAN ALLEN,
H. R. PIERSON,
W. C. LITTLE,
DAVID A. THOMPSON,
THURLOW WEED BARNES,
JOHN E. BRADLEY,
A. B. PRATT,
S. J. BANCROFT,
W. S. PADDOCK,
V. P. HINMAN,
F. C. CALLICUT,
E. NEWCOMB,
DAVID A. THOMPSON,
MARTIN D. CONWAY,
JAMES A. MCKOWAN,
ANSON J. UPSON,
HENRY DARLING,
R. M. TOWNSEND,
ROBT. H. MCLELLAN,
HARVEY J. KING,
M. T. CLOUGH,
WILLIAM KEMP,
CHARLES I. BAKER,
C. L. ALDEN,
J. M. LANDON,
E. F. BULLARD,
R. A. PARMENTER,
H. W. DAY,
C. C. PARMELEE,
A. E. POWERS,
DANIEL D. BUCKLIN, M.D.,
H. B. NIMS & CO.,
GEO. C. BALDWIN,
W. E. KISSELBURGH,
THOMAS COLEMAN,
R. M. HASBROUCK,
CHARLOTTE FOWLER WELLS,
LAURA CARTER HOLLOWAY,
CLEMENCE S. LOZIER, M.D.,
E. B. WHITNEY,
JOSEPHINE SHAW LOWELL,
JULIA A. RAY,
HELEN W. WEBSTER, M.D.,
M. M. EASTMAN,
ANNIE C. HOWLAND, M.D.,
BETSY HART,
LEWIA C. SMITH,
HELEN MILLER,
LAURA G. SHEARMAN,
ELIZABETH CLIFTON,
MARIA M. WELCH,
AMMI CUTTER,
ELIZABETH L. LEWIS,
ZEBULON FERRIS,
JAMES FRAZE GLUCK,
W. R. CURTIS,
ALBERT JONES,
W. C. BRYANT,
JAMES B. & H. B. GREEN,
O. H. MARSHALL,
J. W. TYLER,
DAVID GREY,
THAD. C. DAVIS,
SHELDEN PEASE,
DAVID F. DAY,
A. G. RICE,
L. VAN BOKKELAN,
THEO. F. ROCHESTER, M.D.,
S. SCHEW,
WM. EDWARD FOSTER,
J. C. HARRISON,
GEO. W. TIFFT,
W. D. SHUART,
H. R. SELDEN,
W. MARTIN JONES,
J. SULLIVAN,
SETH H. TERRY,
D. L. CRITTENDEN,
CHAS. E. FITCH,
JAMES B. SHAW,
FRANCIS S. REW,
HARMON C. RIGGS,
WM. CORNING,
D. W. POWERS,
JAMES VICK,
M. B. ANDERSON,
HIRAM SIBLEY,
E. O. HAVEN,
NELSON MILLARD,
MOSES SUMNER,
CARROL E. SMITH,
H. RIEGEL,
CHAS. E. IDE,
W. P. GOODELLE,
GEO. N. KENNEDY,
JOHN L. KING.

"MEMORIAL."

READ BEFORE THE HOUSE JUDICIARY COMMITTEE.

Mr. Chairman and Honorable Gentlemen of the Committee:

As men of intelligence, you cannot be ignorant of the fact that the laws affecting the rights of widows are far from just; that the controlling power over the financial community of interest, existing between husband and wife, is vested solely in the husband; that in law there is no *money* value attached to a woman's services as wife; that, as widow, she has no control over the property which she has helped to earn, save what is delegated by husband or court.

This is a grievous hardship: Therefore I pray that a widow, when not legally disqualified, may be one of the executors of the joint estate accumulated during coverture, whenever she desires to exercise the trust. This change involves no special departure from the present order of things; for every husband has the right to appoint his wife the executor of his will; and if he dies without making a will, the Surrogate enjoys the same privilege. But in no case is the widow allowed an individual voice upon this important subject which affects her so vitally. She occupies the position of a child or an imbecile. Her lips are closed. She is set aside by a legal enactment which refuses to acknowledge that a woman who enters upon a career as wife—leaving, perhaps, a remunerative occupation—earns money in that capacity.

The assumption that women earn no money in wedlock is extremely vicious; because it is based upon the common-law theory of dependence. If property were largely hereditary in this country, as it is in England, it would be different; but it is not. Therefore the simple right of the wife to her separate estate is far from just; for the accumulations of wedlock are still based upon the common law of dependence, instead of upon equity law, with its underlying principles of *independence*.

In the State of New York a husband can convert all real estate into personal and then will it all away from wife and babes—there is no law to restrain him—and he can put testamentary guardians over the persons and property of the minor children. The wife and mother has no more legal voice in the matter than a stranger. The will of the husband is omnipotent.

What are the arguments—if arguments they may be called—against a law that will protect every competent widow in having the careful supervision of her share of the common property—or the husband's property as it is called—*miscalled*, and the guardianship of the *person* of her children? There are three, and it is well there is a trinity, for neither of them has strength enough to stand alone.

First, " A wife earns no money! especially in the upper walks of life where she performs no manual labor, and, per consequence, she should not have a voice in the management of what she has never toiled to acquire." But she superintends the household and bears and rears the children. Motherhood, alone, should secure her this right. A superintendent whose cares are not half as numerous as a housekeeper's are, gets large pay. Suppose a wife lives in a hotel and has no domestic cares, acting as companion, only, to her husband. Is there no money value in companionship? If *I* have a companion who is my peer intellectually and socially, I expect to pay her a handsome sum over and above enough to feed and clothe her with.

A case testing the value of a wife's companionship was recently tried in a court in the State of Ohio. A husband was excommunicated from a society of Mennonites, and the by-laws of that peculiar sect forbade the wife's having any communion with the excommunicant. For a *year* she performed all the duties of housekeeper, but withheld herself as companion. At the end of that time the husband sued the Society and got judgment for $2,500. The value of his wife's companionship was fixed at $208.33⅓ a month, and these people were in the *lower* walks of life. She could not entertain him and his friends with refined deportment, exquisite music, and cultured conversation. *She was a household drudge.*

If the companionship of such an uncultivated wife is valued so highly, what must be the price put upon the companionship of one who has been elegantly educated? one who shines out like a star in *"our best society"?*

Then, again, if there is no money value in the society and companionship of a wife, the law is inconsistent; for it is upon this supposition that it allows the husband heavy " vindictive " damages in compensation for his wife's society, should a third party entice her away from him. Is it usual for single women of culture and refinement to serve as companions for simply their board and clothes? That is all a wife gets for her services unless she is widowed. And then a wife-companion bears children at the risk of her life, and oftentimes at the ruin of her health. *This duty, like love, is priceless.*

It is asked, "How is the widow benefited by being an executor?" I reply, "How is one benefited by having control of one's own business? If one would be well served he must serve himself." If she is not an executor or co-executor, her advice is seldom or never sought in matters in which she alone is most interested. She is left at the mercy of men who best serve their own interest, and

" Mankind is ever weak, and little to be trusted ;
If self the wavering balance strike, it's rarely right adjusted."

The benefit resulting from such a law would be incalculable. You may say, gentlemen, that few widows are qualified to perform the trust. True, undoubtedly, in some cases; but the right to exercise a dormant faculty develops that faculty. Responsibility is one of the greatest educators. Self-reliance and self-government are the spring and source of all real progress. If wives knew that this right could not be wrested from them, they would make themselves intelligent upon the subject. They would keep abreast with financial affairs, and shape their expenditures accordingly, thereby averting many a failure, and by their ready aid and counsel bridge over many a disastrous business chasm. The timely advice of a wife has saved many a man from ruin.

What business firm would expect to prosper if the senior partner refused to counsel with the junior, but allowed him to spend all the money he could get hold of, not knowing a thing about the strength of the bank-account or the success of the enterprise? Would such an establishment prosper? No! And, what is more, no one would expect it to prosper. It would be the laughing-stock of the community where it was located. And yet this is precisely the condition of the marriage relation to-day, and when disaster overtakes it, the blame is too often attached to the innocent.

It is asked, "If you secure the widow an executorship, why not do the same by the children and other *heirs-at-law?*" "For this reason," I reply: "The widow-mother, in most cases, has helped earn the property, and therefore should not be kept on the same plane with her children. The child earns far less than it costs to support it, from the time of birth till it arrives at majority; whereas, women marry at maturity, and spend the prime of their lives in the service of their husbands. They often work more hours a day than the hired servant; and were that labor recompensed as the labor of women other than wives is recompensed, it would secure them a handsome support for their declining years. But the law offers a wife no such recompense; for whatever she earns in the service of the husband belongs to him as absolutely as it did during the period of wife-capture and wife-purchase. Is this just? Should not all persons be protected in their industry? Then, again, the widow is a legal heir to the estate, while the children are not; and she should not be classed with other heirs who have contributed nothing towards the acquirement of the property. Her superior claim is but a just recognition of services rendered. So long as the law invites a husband to set aside his wife, like an imbecile, so long will she be treated like a child, under the cover of protection."

It is a mistaken idea that society will not prosper unless one-half of its adult population is watched over and protected by the other half, at nearly every turn in life. Self-protection is pure gold; whilst restrictive, protective law, as all history demonstrates, is pure dross.

Many prominent judges and lawyers have said to me, "We always advise men, who consult us upon the subject, to appoint their wives their executors, and also advise widows to serve as administrators." Men in the profession understand the value of the position.

Second, "*Disagreement*."—This argument is especially weak; for where there is a family quarrel both parties are to blame. But the product of labor is of the same intrinsic value, whether it is performed in love or hate. I pay my cook the same wages for services, be she amiable or vicious. When I buy a yard of cloth, I do not question the *spirit* of the manufacturers. The value is in the web, not the spirit. The sum of a termagant wife's labor, economy (for a penny saved is as good as a penny earned), and general superintendence of the household, is of the same value in dollars and cents as though she were a paragon of sweetness.

Third, "*Incapacity*."—Here is the mountain that but comparatively few men have had the courage and clear-sightedness to climb over. All the great dead past, that rule the living present, have cried, "Women are imbeciles in business, *especially wives*. All they know about money is how to squander it. They are natural spendthrifts," etc., etc. Now, I have always observed that where money comes hard—and the money of most wives comes *very* hard—that it is spent with thoughtful care. I have found wives far more conservative, in financial matters, than husbands. I speak from practical experience in money-raising for churches and charities. Where the property-status of men and women are equal, a wife will give five dollars where her husband will give five times that amount.

Women will always be the conservatives in finance, so long as they are paid less than men for the same amount of labor equally well done; so long as men occupy all the lucrative positions; and so long as wives have to *beg* for money, which is theirs by every law of justice and equity. When there is no longer sex in law and labor, men and women will be equally generous, equally practicable, and equally capable of managing what belongs to them.

The absolute legal power of the father over the children is as unnatural as it is unjust. I witnessed in Rochester a short time since, the anguish of a Christian mother deprived of the care of her delicate infant daughter, through the will of the husband—*dead*. Judge Selden and other leading lawyers in that city said it was an atrocious law that permitted such things to be. It is only the mother of an illegitimate child who is protected and safe in the possession of her offspring. The humane law denies the virtuous mother—through the will of the father—a right to the personal care and education of her children, *for whom she has suffered as no man can ever suffer.* Even the child is bartered away when it lies in embryo beneath her heart.

Ah! Mr. Chairman, this is a cruel law! A mother is the natural, God-ordained guardian of her offspring; the more tender and self-sacrificing parent, and yet there is not a line of positive law to protect her in the care and ownership of these jewels of her home. Why do not all mothers and just men cry out against such an *iniquitous* law? A wail comes from a widow-mother in Rhode Island saying, "Take my husband's will to the mountain-top and urge all lawmakers to free this nation's records from the shameful story that no mother can control her child unless it is born out of wedlock."

No earthly power should be able to snatch the babe from the mother's breast. Within the last twelve months the walls of a Michigan prison have echoed with the shrieks of a mother, incarcerated for stealing her own babe, the fruit of her womb, blood of her blood, bone of her bone, flesh of her flesh; that which germinated within her body, whose growth and development each day and hour, a portion of her own life was given to perfect. For this she passed through the modern tragedy of child-bed, "and bit back the pain when a man-child was born;" for this she sat out the stars, in sickness, when no eye but her God's was upon her; for this she would give her life as a ransom—if need be; for this she would toil till the back break, and the sinews crack; and yet for unlawfully obtaining possession of this child she was thrown into a felon's cell, "the fittest earthly type of hell,"—and this nation claims to have emerged from barbarism!

In the State of New York a widow has only dower rights, as against the husband's will, in the common property, and in nine cases out of ten a wife has no separate estate. This provision is meager in the extreme, for in the present days of commerce the personal estate is usually much larger than the real. There are thousands of people who own not a foot of land outside the cemetery. In most of the States a widow has a *third* of the net personal property absolutely, which is little enough, for at the husband's death everything comes to a standstill. The estate expires with him, and its body is turned over to the Probate Court for inquisition, and much of its substance is needlessly wasted upon useless routine, and often hopeful estates are entirely consumed in dishonest administration.

A leading daily of New York, says, "If the public only knew the amount that is fleeced out of the estates of widows and orphans by hungry lawyers and dishonest executors every year, there would be a cry of reform which our lawyer-legislators *themselves* would be compelled to hear."

Law, as it now exists, has been found insufficient for the protection of the widow and the fatherless, and this is the *objective point* which I assail, for if we desire to free ourselves from the reproach of injustice and erase from our statutes the rude relics of antiquity, *these laws must be changed.* Probate judges have said to me, "We are powerless to do justice by widows and fatherless children, because we must administer the laws as we find them; we have had no voice in their framing. The system is at fault."

Herein is sounded the key-note of the whole problem. It is the corrupt and corruptable *system* which I denounce. It makes thieves of men who would otherwise be honest. Many a ruined man can trace his first downward step to the settlement of dead men's estates. Many and many a home has been desolated, at the death of a father and husband, by executors and guardians, when, if the widow-mother had risen to her true dignity and crowning as the head of the household, her home and loved ones would not have been scattered to the four winds.

Dumas, *fils,* in speaking to the husband of the wife, says: "Initiate her loyally in your destiny, human and divine, in order that, if you should die before your children be capable of directing themselves, she may not need another *man* to direct them, but may constitute herself father and mother, the loftiest grade to which woman, brought out and developed in her full value, can arrive."

Mr. Chairman, and gentlemen of the Committee, to those honored with a State's trust great responsibilities and duties attach—and great opportunities as well, for advancing human rights and correcting human wrongs. In the light of which I make this prayer, this plea, in behalf of all women who may become widowed, of all children who may become fatherless. The legal changes which I seek to have made, so slight in themselves and yet so potential for good, are but steps onward in individual rights.

It is a sound English doctrine that all rights are created by laws based on expediency, and are alterable, as the public advantage may require, and that the best decisions are the *latest*. Now, it is both expedient and desirable that the law which controls the rights of widows should be altered so as to be in greater harmony with the progressive spirit of the age;

and to this end I have pledged my undying fealty—a fealty to which I am rendering the *best* effort of my life. Bear in mind, gentlemen, that I am aided and abetted in this work by some of the ablest members of the Bar, Press, and Pulpit; by some of the ripest scholars and *literati* in the State; by some of the noblest men and women in this fair land.

Do I expect the bill for the protection of widows to pass? Certainly I do; for between the extremes of conservatism and radicalism there is a class, by no means small, of the alert and sagacious, who respond quickly and heartily to the progress of events. They accept what has been accomplished, turn their backs on the past, and are ready to go forward with the new tasks which are pressing upon them. They are the leaven that quickens the whole mass; and to this element I appeal. If they support the bill, its provisions must be adopted and become the law of New York—a noble precedent, to be quickly followed by other States throughout the Republic.

Very respectfully submitted to the generous consideration of this honorable committee by

Mrs. J. W. Stow.

The bill was introduced in the Senate on the 8th of January, 1879, by Alford Wagstaff, of New York, and referred to the Judiciary Committee. Charles R. Skinner presented it in the Assembly. The House Judiciary granted a "hearing," on which occasion I read the "Memorial" given above. It made just about as much impression on that conservative body as the shadow of a leaf makes on the earth's surface—*just about*. The Committee was largely composed of lawyers; and people are loath to throw water on the fire that warms them. John Bright says, "You might almost as well ask a spider to give up weaving his web, or to destroy that he has woven, as to ask the great body of lawyers to consent to a simplicity and purification of the law."

It mattered not to those gentlemen that the petition was headed by George William Curtis, and followed by hundreds of names, including some of the noblest men and women in the State. The prayer fell on deaf ears and stony ground; for the bill was reported adversely upon. This has been the fate of my bill twice in the Senate of Massachusetts and once in the Legislature of Pennsylvania; but I am not at all discouraged. It is early morning with the effort yet, and the day is long.

THE WIDOW'S PORTION.

CHAPTER 470, LAWS OF NEW YORK.

AN ACT to amend section nine, title three, chapter six, part two of the revised Statutes.

Passed May 18, 1874; three-fifths being present.

The people of the State of New York, represented in Senate and Assembly, do enact as follows:

SECTION 1. Section nine, title third, chapter six, part two of the Revised Statutes is hereby amended so as to read as follows:

§ 9. Where a man having a family shall die, leaving a widow or a minor child or children, the following articles shall not be deemed assets, but shall be included and stated in the inventory of the estate, without being appraised:

1. All spinning-wheels, weaving-looms, one knitting-machine, one sewing-machine, and stoves put up or kept for use by his family.

2. The family Bible, family pictures and school-books, used by or in the family of such deceased person, and books not exceeding in value fifty dollars, which were kept and used as part of the family library, before the decease of such person.

3. All sheep to the number of ten, with their fleeces, and the yarn and cloth manufactured from the same, one cow, two swine, and the pork of such swine, and necessary food for such swine, sheep or cow for sixty days, and all necessary provisions

and fuel for such widow, or child, or children, for sixty days, after the death of such deceased person.

4. All necessary wearing apparel, beds, bedsteads and bedding, necessary cooking utensils, the clothing of the family, the clothes of the widow and her ornaments proper for her station; one table, six chairs, twelve knives and forks, six plates, twelve tea-cups and saucers, one sugar dish, one milk-pot, one tea-pot and twelve spoons, and also other household furniture, which shall not exceed one hundred and fifty dollars in value.

Sec. 4. When a man having a family shall die, leaving a widow or minor child or children, there shall be inventoried by the appraisors and set apart for the use of such widow or for the use of such widow and child or children, or for the use of such child or children, in the manner now prescribed by the ninth Section of Title third, Chapter sixth of Part second of the Revised Statutes, necessary household provisions or other personal property in the discretion of said appraisors, to the value of not exceeding one hundred and fifty dollars, in addition to the articles of personal property now exempt from appraisal by said Section. —1842, Chap. 157, Sec. 2.

DISPOSITION OF MINOR CHILDREN.

Section 1. Every father, whether of full age or a minor, of a child likely to be born, or of any living child under the age of twenty-one years and unmarried, may, by his deed or last will duly executed, dispose of the custody and tuition of such child during its minority, or for any less time, to any person or persons in possession or remainder.—(Sixth edition Revised Statutes, 1875, Vol. 3, page 167.

PROBATE CONFISCATION.

By Mrs. J. W. STOW.

LARGE 12MO, CLOTH, GILT. PRICE $2.00.
PUBLISHED BY THE AUTHOR, AND SOLD BY SUBSCRIPTION.

Address Mrs. STOW, care of FLEMING & Co.,
17 *Franklin St., Boston, Mass.*,
Inclosing P. O. Order for $2.00, and the Book will be mailed immediately, *post-paid*.

THIS is a work of intrinsic value. It touches upon a vital question—the laws affecting the property gathered in wedlock. Ignorance of these laws adds immeasurably to the pauper and criminal classes. It is a book for the home and the fireside. No library is complete without it. It gives the written laws which control dead men's and living widows' estates to-day. It shows the practical working of these laws in the courts. It shows how, under the sounding title of "Justice," the widow and the fatherless are often made a target for thieves. It is written to rouse the popular heart, to stir the dormant reason, to quicken the sense of right, and to get the whole question upon the wave of discussion and investigation.

SHORT EXTRACTS FROM REVIEWS BY THE PRESS.

With the keenness of a cimeter-blade Mrs. Stow dissects the incongruities and useless formalities that for centuries have cumbered the practice of courts, many of which have no further reason for their existence than that the dust of ages has sanctified them.—*Evening Post* (San Francisco).

Mrs. Stow vividly portrays the operations of the law in regard to widows, and cites instances where the whole substance of estates has been swallowed up by post-mortem litigation, and where the red-tape circumlocution, tedious delays, and extraordinary expenses have left nothing for the support of the widow and orphans.—*Los Angeles Express.*

The probate system in all the States is nearly identical, and seems to have been framed with the express purpose of promoting litigation, and enabling parties to become rich by plundering the dead and impoverishing the living. Mrs. J. W. Stow has written a book filled with powerful arguments against this corrupt system, and in support of a much-needed reform. If successful, Mrs. Stow will achieve a greater good for man and woman than has been, or is proposed to be achieved by any of the army of reformers now displaying their banners in the field of progress and advancement.—*Sacramento Bee* (California).

Women who wish to understand what every woman should understand—the laws that most nearly concern their personal interest—should have a copy of this book.—*New North-West* (Portland, Or.).

It is a comfort in these days, when there is so much that is commonplace and tedious in the line of literary issues, to meet with something which bears evidence of having been written with a purpose; whose words come hot from the heart, as it were, and retain their heat after being placed on paper. Such a book is *Probate Confiscation*, whose author is well known to many of our best citizens.—*Boston Transcript.*

The work has a decided value, because it calls attention to a great system of wrong which exists in every State, and which cannot bear the light of day. It should be widely read.—*Woman's Journal* (Boston).

Incidentally the whole system of marriage is considered in its bearings upon women, both in regard to their property and their position generally under existing laws.—*Boston Globe.*

The volume is crammed full of truth, and, to a just man, altogether unpalatable truth. It is an engine, an instrument in a crusade which the author has undertaken—a war which she opens single-handed, but in which she is sure to be soon surrounded with earnest followers. It deserves to be read, for it touches upon subjects which lie close to the heart of every father and mother, every husband and wife, in the land. No loving father wishes to have his children unprovided for and houseless; no loving husband, his wife to be worried to death in courts, appealing and begging for what no one, not even judges, deny to be her honest right. Widows are often treated in probate practice as rebels are in times of rebellion. Confiscation is often the lot of both. Mrs. Stow goes to the root of the subject; and, when she has a hard name to call, she does not mince matters, but "*speaks right* out." It has been a pleasure to read a book with such snap and point to it; and all who take it up will probably agree with us.—*Boston Traveller.*

The work has the merit of frankness and sincere conviction, and of going directly to the point. It should be read to be appreciated.—*Eastern Argus* (Portland, Me.).

Mrs. Stow makes a stirring appeal for the protection of the widow and the fatherless; and all right-minded people must sympathize with her earnest efforts in their behalf.—*Patriot* (Concord, N. H.).

Probate Confiscation is written with a very free pen, and is typographically a very handsome volume.—*Free Press* (Burlington, Vt.).

The author's purpose is, broadly, to improve the condition of women in respect to property-rights; and in this she will have the sympathies of all just men. The work is of more than ordinary merit.—*Hartford Courant* (Conn.).

Mrs. Stow is smart enough to review the whole subject of estates and probates regardless of fear or favor, brave enough to tell the whole truth, and has suffered enough under the system to make her arraignment of the laws and processes of probate stinging and terrible. We wish her Godspeed in her good work. —*Providence Press* (R. I.).

Mrs. Stow exposes the injustice and waste of property during probate adjustment, which ought to go to widows and orphans, in the most glowing light, and makes the reader of her book to sympathize with her and wish her all possible success in her effort to reform our laws. She is going to visit all the northern States and prove what an energetic woman can do for the benefit of widowed women and fatherless children. Her book is full of natural eloquence, combined with piquant illustrative anecdote and warmed up by occasional bitter pungency, that is worth paying for and reading as a literary work without reference to the motive, for it shows remarkable cleverness.—*Evening Bulletin* (Phila., Pa.).

"*Probate Confiscation*" is a spicy, energetic volume. It is a protest and outcry against the injustice of the present probate system, which is the cause of the financial ruin of hundreds of widows and orphans yearly. Mrs. Stow is trying to effect a reform in this direction. Her object is a noble one.—*Buffalo Courier* (N. Y.).

We heartily commend the book as one worthy of careful perusal, and commend the author as an estimable lady, earnestly at work in a most worthy cause.—*Commercial Advertiser* (Buffalo, N. Y.).

The book is informed with zeal and with a vivid conviction of the truths it presents. It abounds in powerful passages which must arrest the attention and quicken the conscience of all who read it. We can heartily commend the work as one calculated to do great good, and as an effective adjunct to the mission to which Mrs. Stow has devoted herself—the reformation of the statutes that deny the natural and equitable rights of women.— *Rochester Democrat* (N. Y.).

Mrs. Stow's pen is dipped in liquid fire. Her words glow and burn over the pages of her book. She shows practical knowledge in the vigorous, fearless manner in which she handles the subjects treated. If women wish to understand their rights under the law, let them purchase and read this book.—*National Citizen* (Syracuse, N. Y.).

Mrs. Stow's account of her long and maddening experience with the "law's delay" is highly interesting, as showing what utter *cussedness* prevails under the mantle of some of our courts of law. It stirs one's hottest wrath to read the author's story, which is told with startling vigor. She calls a spade a spade, and spares not. Many a woman would have sunk into her grave or gone insane under such trials as this lady suffered, but Mrs. Stow is made of sterner stuff. She has not only written this book which holds up the probate court system to the scorn of every person with a sense of justice, but she is laboring to bring about legislative reforms, in the different States, in the manner in which dead men's estates are administered. Such legislation as she is striving to secure deserves prosperity if any cause ever did. Mrs. Stow's book incidentally touches on many of the social questions, and she tells many truths, which are too often avoided by social teachers, in a sharp and forcible manner. The volume deserves general circulation.—*Troy Times* (N. Y.).

Probate Confiscation is a more scathing piece of composition than one often meets with. Mrs. Stow certainly makes out a strong case against the probate laws as usually administered; and no argument for their repeal could be stronger than her own story as she tells it.—*Albany Evening Journal* (N. Y.).

The book is written in a style differing materially from the productions of ordinary authors. The language made use of is that of an injured woman possessed of ability to paint the picture of women's wrongs. Mrs. Stow speaks with a frankness that is refreshing. While her arguments are clothed in good language her words are of burning significance. The work is one which will greatly interest every *woman*. Mrs. Stow has entered upon a crusade in behalf of women, in which she needs the united support and encouragement of her sex.—*Albany Knickerbocker* (N. Y.).

Mrs. Stow has shown much true literary talent in her book *Probate Confiscation*. It exhibits great cleverness and humor in an unobjectionable way.—*Albany Law Journal* (N. Y.).

The *third* edition of this book is proof of its merit with the class of readers to whom the graver subjects of a legal and moral kind are of interest. The volume is not intended to tickle the fancy or to please the prejudices of any class. The writer sets her face against the wrong and injustice of the probate law with the energy and zeal of one who has been scourged by the system. Her manner of attack may not be admired, but the undertone of honest conviction, of personal knowledge gained from a disastrous wrong suffered from the weakness and shortcoming of this law, is plain.—*Brooklyn Eagle* (N. Y.).

After carefully reading *Probate Confiscation* we give it our hearty endorsement and Godspeed. Mrs. Stow's appeal for the protection of the widow and fatherless is one which should arouse the sympathy of all fair-minded people.—*New York Palladium*.

Mrs. Stow recites the story of her wrong with passionate eloquence.—*New York Tribune*.

The book will not be found hard reading. It is no "kiss the rod" affair. It is a swift burning word, the inspiration of a passionate heart, the "*no*" of a strong will outraged in the holiest instincts of affection and justice.—*Home Journal* (New York).

www.ingramcontent.com/pod-product-compliance
Lightning Source LLC
Chambersburg PA
CBHW022053230426
43672CB00008B/1161